Fact or Fiction?

| Mediums

Other Titles in the Fact or Fiction? Series:

Alien Abductions

Ape-Men

Astrology

Faith Healing

Fortune Telling

Haunted Houses

Life After Death

Mysterious Monsters

Psychics

UFOs

Voodoo

Werewolves

Fact or Fiction?

| Mediums

Jen Hirt, Book Editor

GREENHAVEN PRESS

An imprint of Thomson Gale, a part of The Thomson Corporation

THOMSON

———✦———™

GALE

133.91
MED

Detroit • New York • San Francisco • New Haven, Conn. • Waterville, Maine • London

Christine Nasso, *Publisher*
Elizabeth Des Chenes, *Managing Editor*

© 2007 Thomson Gale, a part of The Thomson Corporation.

Thomson and Star logo are trademarks and Gale and Greenhaven Press are registered trademarks used herein under license.

For more information, contact:
Greenhaven Press
27500 Drake Rd.
Farmington Hills, MI 48331-3535
Or you can visit our Internet site at http://www.gale.com

LIBRARY OF CONGRESS CATALOGING-IN-PUBLICATION DATA

Mediums / Jen Hirt, book editor.
  p. cm. -- (Fact or fiction)
Includes bibliographical references and index.
ISBN-13: 978-0-7377-3509-3 (hardcover : alk. paper)
ISBN-10: 0-7377-3509-0 (hardcover : alk. paper)
1. Mediums. 2. Psychic ability. I. Hirt, Jen, 1975–
BF1286.M43 2006
133.9'1--dc22
                                                    2006022937

Printed in the United States of America
10 9 8 7 6 5 4 3 2 1

Contents

Foreword   7

Introduction   9

Chapter 1: The Evidence in Support of Mediums

1. Mediums Communicate Directly with the Dead   16
   David Fontana

2. Mediums Help the Dead and the Living Connect   29
   Suzane Northrop

3. Mediums Are Part of the Spiritualist Religion   39
   John Walliss

4. Mediums Have Passed Scientific Tests   56
   Gary E. Schwartz

5. Mediums Understand How Spirits Communicate   69
   James Van Praagh

Chapter 2: The Evidence Against Mediums

1. *The Skeptic's Dictionary* Explains Claims Against Mediums   81
   Robert T. Carroll

2. Mediums Are Frauds   97
   Joe Nickell

3. Proof of Mediums' Abilities Is Flawed   109
   Richard Wiseman and Ciaran O'Keefe

4. Television Mediums Are Not Authentic   119
   James Underdown

5. Mediums Are Skilled Speakers   129
   Robin Wooffitt

Epilogue: Analyzing the Evidence   151

Glossary   163
For Further Research   166
Index   171

Foreword

"There are more things in heaven and earth, Horatio, than are dreamt of in your philosophy."

—*William Shakespeare,*
Hamlet

"Extraordinary claims require extraordinary evidence."

—*Carl Sagan,*
The Demon-Haunted World

Almost every one of us has experienced something that we thought seemed mysterious and unexplainable. For example, have you ever known that someone was going to call you just before the phone rang? Or perhaps you have had a dream about something that later came true. Some people think these occurrences are signs of the paranormal. Others explain them as merely coincidence.

As the examples above show, mysteries of the paranormal ("beyond the normal") are common. For example, most towns have at least one place where inhabitants believe ghosts live. People report seeing strange lights in the sky that they believe are the spaceships of visitors from other planets. And scientists have been working for decades to discover the truth about sightings of mysterious creatures like Bigfoot and the Loch Ness monster.

There are also mysteries of magic and miracles. The two often share a connection. Many forms of magical belief are tied to religious belief. For example, many of the rituals and beliefs of the voodoo religion are viewed by outsiders as magical practices. These include such things as the alleged Haitian voodoo practice of turning people into zombies (the walking dead).

There are mysteries of history—events and places that have been recorded in history but that we still have questions about today. For example, was the great King Arthur a real king or merely a legend? How, exactly, were the pyramids built? Historians continue to seek the answers to these questions.

Then, of course, there are mysteries of science. One such mystery is how humanity began. Although most scientists agree that it was through the long, slow process of evolution, not all scientists agree that indisputable proof has been found.

Subjects like these are fascinating, in part because we do not know the whole truth about them. They are mysteries. And they are controversial—people hold very strong and opposing views about them.

How we go about sifting through information on such topics is the subject of every book in the Greenhaven Press series Fact or Fiction? Each anthology includes articles that present the main ideas favoring and challenging a given topic. The editor collects such material from a variety of sources, including scientific research, eyewitness accounts, and government reports. In addition, a final chapter gives readers tools to analyze the articles they read. With these tools, readers can sift through the information presented in the articles by applying the methods of hypothetical reasoning. Examining these topics in this way adds a unique aspect to the Fact or Fiction? series. Hypothetical reasoning can be applied to any topic to allow a reader to become more analytical about the material he or she encounters. While such reasoning may not solve the mystery of who is right or who is wrong, it can help the reader separate valid from invalid evidence relating to all topics and can be especially helpful in analyzing material where people disagree.

Introduction

A psychic medium is a person who claims to be a messenger between the living and the dead. Mediums communicate these messages in a variety of ways—through séances, by dream interpretation, during private consultations, or in front of television cameras and studio audiences. One modern medium, Yvonne Limoges, said that "I can see and hear spirits and they use me to do writings and communicate through me at what we call a 'spirit session.'"[1] Many others like Limoges make similar claims, and their popularity has grown in recent years, especially on television. For example, journalist Anne Becker reported in 2006 that "After the recent success of scripted series dealing with telepathy, such as NBC's *Medium* and the WB's *Supernatural,* cable networks like Court TV, Sci Fi and WE [Women's Entertainment] are programming psychic-themed reality shows."[2] Even though mediums' abilities make good entertainment, their claims fall outside mainstream science. Does that reveal a limitation with science, or does it mean that mediums are hucksters?

Humans have always been curious about death—from Native American shamans to Egyptian tombs and Viking burial ships. Shamans held exulted places in their tribes because their connections to the deceased could bring wisdom, luck, and prophecy. Ancient Egyptians built elaborate pyramid tombs filled with riches. They believed that the dead pharaoh would need possessions in the afterlife. Vikings held similar beliefs, but rather than building pyramids, they buried entire ships with their dead comrades laid inside so they would have vessels in the next world. Reverence for the dead and subsequent actions that presumed an afterlife defined those cultures.

These days, we remain curious and reverent, but we are also anxious. Despite advances in science and medicine, we don't know what death is like, nor do we know for certain if a unique personality survives. Given all we *do* know, it's tough to admit we still *don't know* something. Do mediums take advantage of this anxiety?

Religion gives us the spiritual basis for hoping that another world awaits. But for many people, it is mediums who continue to offer what appears to be extraordinary evidence.

Seeking Reassurance Through Mediums

So, what *do* mediums provide for us? To start to answer that question, first be aware that mediumship has changed over time; mediums in different eras have provided different phenomena. The modern era of mediums began in 1858, when Kate and Margaret Fox claimed a spirit was in their Hydesville, New York, house. The entity rapped on the walls in response to questions. The sisters later confessed to a hoax, then recanted their confession, leaving the episode muddied and dubious. But the concept had entered the American mind. "Five years after the Hydesville Rappings, there were, by one estimate, no fewer than thirty thousand mediums, professional and amateur, in America alone."[3] In England, mediums engaged in all sorts of phenomena—tipping tables, producing voices or ectoplasm, and generating orbs of light. All, it was said, came from the spirit world.

Messages from dead relatives didn't become a standard part of mediumship until after World War I. Survivors, when faced with the staggering loss of life and subsequent distrust in a society that allowed such carnage, turned to mediums for comfort. Later, spiritualist camps popped up in America. These were utopian villages entirely devoted to mediums. Mediums made up the residents, the government, and the employees; commerce was centered on mediums charging tourists for readings. Some are still in operation, such as Lily Dale, New York, and Cassadaga, Florida. In the 1960s and 1970s, New Age channelers claimed to contact every spirit from ancient warriors to space aliens to dolphins. The 1990s saw the evolution of television mediums working with a studio audience. Most recently, the 2006 network television lineup featured two prime-time dramas based on the lives of actual mediums, and a cable network produced a 2006 show where mediums claimed to contact rock music legend John Lennon (lead singer of the 1960s group The Beatles).

Interest in mediums comes and goes in phases. For example, the immensely popular show *Crossing Over With John Edward* was a favorite on the SciFi cable channel, but it was cancelled in 2004. Two years later, Edward returned to cable with a new show and a new format. He scrapped his fast-paced readings of a few members in a large audience and instead opted for seminars followed by private visits to homes, where he follows up on the accuracy of messages he gave at seminars. The new show, which premiered on the WE [Women's Entertainment] channel in March 2006, is called *John Edward Cross Country.* "Sometimes it feels like catching up with an old friend," he says. "And it doesn't feel like 'John Edward the psychic medium' asking the questions; it's John the person."[4]

Mediums provide connection, reassurance, and closure, which is perhaps what has made modern mediums like John Edward, Alison Dubois, and James Van Praagh into celebrities. When you think about a loved one who has died, do you wonder what their final thoughts were, or what they would have said to you, given the chance? How far would you go to find out? Coming to a comfortable understanding of a difficult event is what is meant by *closure.* No one, be they hardened skeptics or devout believers, would deny that closure is important. But a controversy brews when people debate exactly *how* to achieve closure, especially when it comes to mediums. Edward has said that despite his abilities, "mediumship is not a cure for grief. I can't fix things for you. I can make it better, but I can't fix it."[5] The Spiritist religion, which advocates mediumship as a main part of their doctrine, does not support mediums acting alone or charging for services. "We educate and orient our mediums for a sacred duty and concentrate on the teaching of morality."[6] From another viewpoint comes psychotherapist Jane Greer, who calls her private medium abilities "transcommunication." She noted that after her mother died, the mother was "connecting with me through energy, animal visitations, music, and dreams."[7] These differing viewpoints fall into further contention when the topic of evidence comes up.

The Problem of Evidence

Mediums have encountered the most resistance in the realm of evidence. In your opinion, does a private account hold more weight than rigorous and repeated scientific experiments? The articles you are about to read cover the spectrum of evidence, from anecdotal to religious to scientific. As you read, consider these questions: What do you think is suitable evidence of communication from the spirit world? Who has the credibility to support or debunk supernatural powers? You'll notice that skeptics draw attention to what mediums *haven't* done, whereas mediums draw attention to the private, personal testimonies of people who benefited from a reading. Skeptic Michael Shermer argued that "Like all other animals, we humans evolved to connect the dots between events so as to discern patterns meaningful for our survival. Like no other animals, we tell stories about the patterns we find. Sometimes the patterns are real; sometimes they are illusions."[8] Shermer suggests paying careful attention to what might be an illusion, especially if you are in a grief-stricken state, and thus vulnerable to manipulation.

Psychotherapist Jane Greer agreed that grief can make one vulnerable to "psychological tricks. . . . As things began to happen, I of course wondered if they could, indeed, be a product of my imagination. But the sheer volume, however, as well as the repetitive nature and specificity, of the signs I've received since [my mother's] death has been a validation of a connection that goes beyond my own desire."[9]

Why Learn About Mediums?

Prior to coming across this book, you may not have ever thought about the significance of learning about mediums. There are certainly more pressing global issues demanding your attention. However, there are good reasons for learning the arguments for and against mediums.

If mediums are fakes, then many people have been duped out of money (for a ticket to a reading, for travel expenses to a seminar, to buy a book, to subscribe to a newsletter). They've also been tricked into believing a loved one is still around, in spirit. Monetary loss can be recouped, but emotional damage from deception is not so easily healed. Doubters are skeptical of the instant gratification mediums offer to desperate people. Learning how grieving people are susceptible to scams is an important step in the development of your critical thinking skills.

But if mediums are real, we have a tremendous amount of rethinking to do—about religion, about the laws of psychics, and about grief and forgiveness. We would also have to reconsider justice and punishment. For example, if a murder victim contacted a medium and revealed the killer's identity, how would our current court system have to change in order to accommodate such evidence? Or, consider this: If credible experiments prove that mediums are real, should we have a say in how mediums use their abilities? Some might argue that mediums have a moral obligation to solve crimes and mysteries, and that their abilities should not be left to the whims and financial bottom-lines of television channels, best-seller lists, and flashy Web sites.

Every author in this book would probably agree that we haven't learned everything there is to know, and science has its limits. We would be fools to dismiss new claims right away. Intelligent thinkers such as early twentieth-century philosopher William James and mystery author Sir Arthur Conan Doyle studied mediums and concluded they were real. And there is no doubt that many people who went to a reading came away feeling relieved; a message from a loved one may have changed their lives for the better. Could spiritual awareness be more important than scientific verification? The viewpoints you are about to read will answer these questions, raise others, and will hopefully provide a sound foundation for studying the intriguing world of afterlife communication.

References

1. Yvonne Limoges, "I am a Spiritist," *The Journal of Religion and Psychical Research*, July 2005, p. 122.
2. Anne Becker, "Psyched About Psychics; Cable is stocking up on supernatural reality," *Broadcasting and Cable*, January 30, 2006, p. 14.
3. *Mysteries of the Unknown: Spirit Summoning*. Alexandria, Virginia: Time-Life Books, 1989, p. 22.
4. Quoted in Kate O'Hare, "John Edward Takes the Other Side Coast to Coast," *The Buffalo News*, March 12, 2006, final edition, p. TV2.
5. O'Hare, "John Edward Takes the Other Side Coast to Coast, " p. TV2.
6. Limoges, "I am a Spiritist," p. 125.
7. Jane Greer, *The Afterlife Connection*. New York: St. Martin's Press, 2003, p. 26.
8. Michael Shermer, "Deconstructing the Dead," *Scientific American*, August 2001, p. 29.
9. Greer, *The Afterlife Connection*, pp. 28–29.

Fact or Fiction?

CHAPTER 1

The Evidence in Support of Mediums

Mediums Communicate Directly with the Dead

David Fontana

In this viewpoint, British writer David Fontana contends that mediums communicate with the dead. Through that lens, he reconsiders some history and analyzes skeptical arguments, pointing out their weaknesses.

Fontana believes that the Western world's way of thinking, as put forth by "materialistic brain scientists," as he calls them, does not allow for the existence of mediums and therefore needs to change. He uses the example of Socrates to reevaluate assumptions about mental illness. He asserts that history shows that mediums are communicating directly with the dead.

David Fontana has a doctorate in psychology. He has held a number of teaching positions in the United Kingdom and Europe and is the author of twenty-six books.

Mediumship has been defined in a number of different ways, but basically it is the alleged ability to receive communications from people who have died. There is an important distinction between mediums and psychics.... While mediums claim to be in touch with the spirit world, psychics are confined to information from this world, which they claim to gather telepathically, clairvoyantly, or precognitively. Many mediums take the view that all those with mediumistic gifts are also psychic, but insist it is possible to have psychic gifts without being mediumistic. This is probably true. Old style fortune-tellers now refer to themselves as psychics, and many of them use a wide range of paraphernalia to help them in their work, including Tarot Cards, Rune Stones, Crystal Balls and the I Ching. By contrast, mediums rarely use physical aids of this kind, relying instead on what the spirits tell them, either directly or through a so-called spirit guide, who is usually someone who claims to have lived once on earth, but not always. Frequently these guides are described as Native Americans or as ancient Chinese sages, and the explanation given for this is that both these cultural groups followed paths (Shamanism and Taoism respectively) that connected not only to the spirit world but to the sacredness of the natural world. The resulting deep-seated spiritual harmony which they enjoyed between heaven and earth gives them a special facility to work with mediums, a facility not shared by other advanced spirits, who, it is said, find it difficult to lower their vibrations sufficiently to penetrate the dense matter of which the physical planes are composed.

The mediumistic gift expresses itself in a number of different ways, from purely mental mediumship at one end of the scale, with the medium consciously relaying messages supposedly from the deceased, to physical mediumship at the other, in which the medium, usually in deep trance, is said to supply a form of subtle energy that is used by the spirits to produce psychokinetic effects. It is often said that all mediumistic gifts first manifest themselves in early childhood, though they may lay dormant in the face of parental disapproval and emerge again later in life, typically as a consequence of working with a development circle run by an experienced medium who helps students (often through meditation and visualization practices) to lower the boundaries between the conscious and the unconscious mind, thus allowing the elusive whispers from the spirit world received at the level of the latter to emerge into consciousness. Importantly, the development circle also tries to help the budding medium to know how to raise these barriers when needed, so that he or she is not 'invaded' by unwanted and possibly ill-intentioned spirits.

Mediumship appears to be at least as old as recorded history, and in early times was often thought to be an indication of contact with the gods. Space does not allow a survey of this historical background ..., so let us take just one example, drawing it from the cradle of Western civilization and from one of the wisest men of his time, namely Socrates (469–399 B.C.). Plato gives us a good description of Socrates' relationship with his daemon (from the Greek *daimon*, a word meaning god or indwelling spirit, and not to be confused with 'demon,' a medieval corruption of the true meaning of the term prompted by the belief that anything not sanctioned by the church was evil). We are told that Socrates would go into a spontaneous trance and remain in rapt contemplation, sometimes for hours and once for a whole day and night, during which he would consult this guiding spirit. On occasions it would break into his thoughts and even his conversation, and as he said himself it would oppose him even about trifles if he was about to make a mistake of some kind, often stopping him in the middle of a speech. Its silence when he was leaving his house to attend the court that sentenced him to death and while he was addressing the judges led him to announce that 'what has happened to me is a good (and not a mistake), and those of us who think that death is an evil are in error.' Spurning the opportunity to escape the death penalty, passed on him for allegedly not worshipping the State gods and for corrupting the young with his new religious ideas, Socrates calmly drank the fatal dose of hemlock, and without regrets left the physical world. ...

What would modern medicine make of Socrates' experiences if he was on earth today? In all probability they would be diagnosed as psychotic, and Socrates would be labeled a borderline schizophrenic, subject to an hallucinatory inner voice that he mistakenly credited with independent existence and that interfered with his ability to live a normal life (thus, although Socrates saw the intellect as interfering with his inner voice, modern medicine would see it as the other way round). Socrates would be prescribed drug therapy to put matters right, and materialistic brain scientists would subject him to brain scans to identify which areas of his brain were active when he heard his voice, and subsequently insist that everything was due to cerebral malfunction. This dogmatic approach to inner experience can be highly misleading because it represents a form of circular reasoning. The materialist psychiatrist decides to label mediumistic voices such as those of Socrates as mental illness, and then proceeds to explain them away as mental illness. The materialist brain scientist decides to label them as brain malfunction and then proceeds to explain them away as brain malfunction. The impression of scientific infallibility given by materialistic psychiatrists and brain scientists often serves to lend their pronouncements the aura of holy writ, seemingly disqualifying the layperson from having anything worth saying on the nature of his or her own mental life. Just as once the multitudes were persuaded by the priesthood they had no right to approach the divine except through the intermediation of the church, so the multitudes are now persuaded by the materialistic creed of our times that they have no right to approach mental life except through the intermediation of those who put their faith in prescription drugs and brain scans.

We can go further and say that not only is the dogmatic approach by materialistic science to the mysteries of the human mind misleading, it reveals a disturbing ignorance. Ignorance is not so much the act of not knowing something, as it is the act of not knowing something but claiming to know. The materialistic scientist would have us believe that he 'knows' that any claimed inner spiritual experience has nothing to do with spirituality—since he has already decided that spirituality, along with psychic abilities, does not exist—and has everything to do with mental illness and the human powers of self-delusion. Lacking any personal acquaintance with inner spiritual or psychic experiences, the materialistic scientist 'knows' that those who have such experiences are wrong in their interpretation of them, while he or she is of course right. . . . If we tell ourselves often enough that we cannot do something, then usually we cannot do it. Our prophecy of our own failure becomes self-fulfilling. At a much deeper level, if we tell ourselves that there is no spiritual dimension to existence, there is no intuitive wisdom that can tell us more about ourselves than can our textbooks, there are no psychic abilities in ourselves or in others and no possibility of contact with the deceased, then all these negatives become part of our thinking, and cause us to shut out the possibility of experiencing any or all of these things. . . .

The Super-ESP Argument

The skeptic is therefore always able to claim that what is called sensory leakage from the physical world (word of mouth, written records, etc.) rather than communications from the deceased can explain the information obtained through the medium. In the context of survival, sensory leakage implies that there must be some channel, no matter how seemingly incredible, which allows information to reach the medium through her normal senses, thus obviating the need to propose the existence of communications from the dead. But suppose that communications through a medium produced information that is so unlikely to be due to sensory leakage that no unbiased observer would accept it as an explanation, and suppose that the medium obtains such communications consistently and over many sittings with many different people, will this put the issue beyond doubt? Once more, unfortunately not, for at this point the Super-ESP argument is likely to be introduced. . . .

The Super-ESP (or Super-PSI) argument has it that all the information obtained through mediums could come not from the deceased but from sources on earth. They may receive it telepathically from the mind of the sitter (even though the latter may not be consciously thinking about the information at the time), telepathically from the minds of people elsewhere, clairvoyantly from the environment, or even precognitively from the future moment when the sitter checks on the facts given in the communications and finds them to be correct. The term Super-ESP was coined by Hornell Hart in 1959, but the concept had already been developed by [Frank] Podmore in a number of his writings, and it was spelled out later in more detail by Charles Richet. The theory has proved attractive not only to Richet but to many others. For example, [Professor J.B.] Rhine considered that there is nothing on record from mediums 'that cannot be explained by the sort of omnibus hypothesis' [i.e., Super-ESP] into which we have expanded the old counter-hypothesis of telepathy (Rhine 1949), while Professor E.R. Dodds argued that Super-ESP accounts for the limited degree of relevance and continuity in most trance communications (Dodds 1934). In other words, the medium is picking up a range of information by Super-ESP and gives it all to the sitter, not knowing what is relevant to him or her and what is not. In further support of Super-ESP, Professor Gardner Murphy put it that we have direct evidence for the ability of good psychics to 'filch' evidence from the minds of living people (Murphy 1945). . . .

It is true that we do have apparent evidence for spontaneous telepathy and clairvoyance among the living, but there are few examples that yield the kind of detailed evidence sometimes acquired through mediumship. It is also true that some commentators consider poltergeist phenomena to be associated exclusively with the living, but it is by no means certain that they are correct in this. . . . What other spontaneous cases might we take into account as unequivocal evidence of ESP from the living? Death-bed visions? Hardly. The majority of these visions, seen by the dying and sometimes by those at the bedside, are recognized by the dying as deceased relatives and friends who, it is said, have come to help their transition to the next world (Barrett 1988, Morse and Perry 1994, Bozzano 1998). Furthermore, in many cases the appearance of these visions is greeted with surprise by both the dying and the bystanders, suggesting that their own ESP abilities do not appear to be involved.

More Evidence Against Super-ESP

Another argument favored by some supporters of Super-ESP is that we have no warrant to suppose that if one paranormal performance is difficult for a living mind, the many performances required by that mind if it is to obtain the detailed information given by mediums must be out of the question. [Stephen E.] Braude in particular considers 'It may be enough [for a living mind] merely to wish for something to happen, and then it does.' It may simply be sufficient to have a need or make a wish under efficacious circumstances, and 'virtually anything at all can happen ... *Task complexity may simply not be an issue*'. He uses the term 'magic wand' to describe this supposed ability—one simply expresses a wish under the right circumstances, and all ESP abilities operate together to bring it to fruition. This is an interesting idea. Paranormal abilities in the living may indeed all derive from a common source, ensuring that all can be used in conjunction with each other as well as individually. But are we seriously to suppose that if mediums have this ability they would be unable to use it to recognize that their information is coming from the living rather than from the dead? If it may be 'enough merely to wish for something to happen, and then it does' as Braude suggests, surely mediums have only to wish to know the source of their evidence in order to know it—or are we supposed to believe that they do in fact know it and have all been deliberately misleading us over a century or more with their talk of spirits?

Furthermore, what evidence is there that living beings with ESP abilities, even if used in concert, can in fact achieve paranormal effects or obtain paranormal knowledge comparable in quality and extent to that associated with mediumship? For example, . . . experiments by Roy and Robertson (2001), Robertson and Roy (2001) and by Schwartz and his various colleagues (2001, 2001, 2002) yield evidence that gifted mediums are able to obtain accurate information, ostensibly from the deceased, for sitters who are concealed from them by screens and of whose identity they have no idea. Have we evidence, under similarly controlled conditions, that ESP by the living can produce comparable results? It is for supporters of the 'magic wand' theory to prove that they can by setting up similar experiments using those who claim only psychic abilities rather than mediumship. It should not be difficult to do this. However, there is no evidence as yet that they have made the attempt.

The possible existence of Super-ESP cannot be refuted, and in theory it remains conceivable that any evidence for survival [of the soul in the afterlife] could be explained away as originating in the psychic abilities of the living. However, my experience of mediumship began over 35 years ago, and during these years I have sat with and interviewed any number of mediums and sitters and those reporting spontaneous cases. To date, I have not met anyone (including myself) who has thought it appropriate to attribute highly significant veridical information received through mediums to Super-ESP rather than to survival. . . .

Another argument against the Super-ESP explanation is that sometimes the information given by the medium has not been in the sitter's conscious mind for many years, and no feasible explanation has yet been offered as to how the medium can unconsciously rummage through obscure areas of a recipient's unconscious in order to come upon it, or on what basis and by what method she can then select it as relevant from the mass of competing information held in the unconscious. Dodds' (1934) suggestions that rummaging is unnecessary because the emotional charge that the material holds for the sitter may render it particularly accessible to the medium seems to me unconvincing in that many of the facts that come through mediums, although accurate, carry little emotional charge for the sitter at the time. They may be small, relatively inconsequential things, and their significance as indicative of survival may not be apparent to the sitter until they have been confirmed at some later date. Many sitters have told me that they had in their conscious minds many far more relevant and emotionally charged facts that they hoped might come through the medium than those that actually did, and were surprised that the former were neglected in favor of the latter. Another argument against Dodds' suggestion is that although some of the details that come through a medium may have little or no emotional appeal at the time for the sitter, they may have strong emotional appeal for the communicator, and it may be this that determines why they come through. . . .

Rethinking the Super-ESP Assumption

Braude (2003) puts forward a different argument to suggest that the medium may not have to rummage through obscure areas of the sitter's mind in order to get her information, namely that we have 'no warrant for imposing any limits on the scope and functioning of paranormal abilities.' Thus although the information produced by mediums may appear so obscure that it stretches credibility to suppose it could be the result of Super-ESP, our conception of what is and what is not obscure applies only 'to normal methods of acquiring information . . . we're in no position to insist that normally obscure information is also psychically obscure.' The answer to this is that there is no unequivocal evidence that our conception of what is obscure does not apply. . . .

Supporters of Super-ESP have also provided no feasible explanation of how the medium, if she gains her information by precognizing the future moment when the sitter checks up and finds the information to be correct, can select the relevant future events from the countless others competing for the attention of her supposed precognitive abilities. Furthermore, supporters of Super-ESP have not explained why, if precognition is the explanation, the information the medium gives to sitters frequently bears little resemblance to the actual future events surrounding its confirmation. . . .

Conclusions on Super-ESP

The final reason why Super-ESP fails to qualify as an adequate alternative to survival is that it is an hypothesis that cannot be falsified. That is, there is no set of circumstances in which we can effectively test whether it is false or not (as [philosopher] Karl Popper made clear, such circumstances are an imperative before a theory can be regarded as scientific). In effect, the supporters of Super-ESP are claiming that, as we do not know the extent of what can be achieved by psychic abilities, it is theoretically possible that clairvoyance, precognition, and telepathy from the living can therefore explain all communications from supposed discarnates. But how can we test this claim in the absence of measures capable of establishing the extent of psychic abilities? No such measures exist. The Super-ESP hypothesis depends upon what 'may be the right explanation if only it were possible to know enough to prove it.' Such a form of reasoning would be summarily rejected if it was advanced in any other context. One cannot construct an hypothesis or even a sound argument on such a basis. I am aware of the argument that survival is itself an hypothesis that cannot be falsified since we cannot prove that survival does not exist. But proving that something does not exist is not what is meant by falsifying an hypothesis. We cannot prove that anything, even a unicorn, does not exist. An hypothesis is therefore falsified either by showing that it does not effectively fit the known facts, or that there are other theories that fit them much better. Unless we reject the concept of survival on principle, it can be argued that it fits the known facts of many of the cases in the literature better than does the Super-ESP theory, since the latter relies upon the extra assumption that ESP may be very much more powerful than has so far been demonstrated in the laboratory, whereas survival depends upon the evidence actually given as part of the information that comes through mediums. Why should much of this information prove to be correct, whereas the repeated assurance that it comes from the deceased, which forms such an integral part of it, always be incorrect? And if incorrect, why should mediums always be deceived into believing it?

Finally, even if the Super-ESP explanation could be shown to be true, it would by no means destroy the case for survival. In fact it could be argued that it would support it in that it would reveal that the mind has a quite extraordinary ability to operate outside time and space. . . . For example, supporters of Super-ESP tell us that in proxy sittings, when the sitter does not have in mind the information the medium is communicating and this information cannot therefore be taken telepathically from his or her mind, the medium can acquire it telepathically from the mind of somebody elsewhere in the world who has it. The person may be nearby or thousands of miles away. Space it seems is no problem for the medium's hypothetical Super-ESP ability. Where no one living has the information, the Super-ESP theory has it that the medium gleans it clairvoyantly from wherever it happens physically to exist. This of course may again be many hundreds or thousands of miles away. Once more, space seems to be no problem. . . .

As already discussed, the Super-ESP hypothesis has now been expanded to suggest that instead of obtaining evidence from the mind of the deceased, the medium can precognitively access the moment in time when the sitter acknowledges the evidence as correct, or the evidence is discovered somewhere in the physical world. If this were true, it implies the medium has extraordinary Super-ESP abilities that operate outside time. Which brings us back once more to the point that if some part of the mind can operate intelligently outside time and space, we have a strong case for arguing that part of the mind at least survives the death of the physical body.

References

1. Sir W. Barrett, *Death-Bed Visions*. 1926. Reprint, London: Aquarian, 1988.
2. E. Bozzano, *Phénomenes Psychique au Moment de la Mort*. 1923. Reprint, Paris: JMG, 1998.
3. R. Brandon, *The Spiritualists*. London: Weidenfeld & Nicolson, 1982.
4. S.E. Braude, *Immortal Remains*. New York: Rowman & Littlefield, 2003.
5. S. Brown, *The Heyday of Spiritualism*. New York: Hawthorn, 1970.
6. W. Crookes, *The Phenomena of Spiritualism*. London: James Burns, 1874.
7. E.R. Dodds, "Why I Do Not Believe in Survival," *Proceedings of the Society for Psychical Research*, no. 42, 1934.
8. L. Dossey, *Healing Beyond the Body*. London: TimeWarner, 2002.
9. A. Douglas, *Extrasensory Powers: A Century of Psychical Research*. London: Victor Gollancz, 1976.
10. Lord Dowding, *Lychgate*. London: Rider, 1945.
11. Sir A. Conan Doyle, *History of Spiritualism*. 2 vols, 1926. Reprint. London: Psychic, 1989.
12. D. Fontana, "Evidence Inconsistent with the Super-ESP Theory," *Journal of the Society for Psychical Research*, no. 63, 1999.
13. E.J. Garrett, *Many Voices: The Autobiography of a Medium*. New York: Putnam, 1968.
14. H.G. Jackson, *The Spirit Rappers*. New York: Doubleday, 1972.
15. D. Lorimer, *Survival? Body, Mind and Death in the Light of Psychic Experience*. London: Routledge & Kegan Paul, 1984.
16. J. Mishlove, *The Roots of Consciousness*. New York: Random House, 1975.
17. R. Moore, *In Search of White Crows*. New York: Oxford University Press, 1977.
18. M. Morse and P. Perry, *Parting Visions*. London: Piatkus, 1994.
19. G. Murphy, "An Outline of Survival Evidence," *Journal of the American Society for Physical Research*, 1945.
20. A. Owen, *The Darkened Room*. London: Virago, 1989.
21. I.M. Owen and M. Sparrow, *Conjuring Up Philip: An Adventure in Psychokinesis*. New York: Harper and Row, 1976.
22. R.D. Owen, *Footfalls on the Boundary of Another World*. London: Trubner, 1860.
23. J.B. Rhine, "Precognition Reconsidered," *Journal of Parapsychology*, no. 9, 1949.
24. C. Richet, *Thirty Years of Psychical Research*. Trans. S. de Bratt. London: Collins, 1923.
25. T.J. Robertson and T.J. Roy, "A Preliminary Study of the Acceptance by Non-Recipients of Medium's Statement to Recipients," *Journal of the Society for Psychical Research*, vol. 65, no. 2, 2001.

26. A. Roy and T. Robertson, "A Double-Blind Procedure for Assessing the Relevance of a Medium's Statements to a Recipient," *Journal of the Society for Psychical Research*, vol. 65, no. 3, 2001.

27. G.E.R. Schwartz and G.S. Russek, "Evidence of Anomalous Information Retrieval Between Two Mediums: Telepathy, Network Memory Resonance, and Continuance of Consciousness," *Journal of the Society for Psychical Research*, vol. 65, no. 4, 2001.

28. G.E.R. Schwartz, G.S. Russek, and C. Barentsen, "Accuracy and Replicability of Anomalous Information Retrieval: Replication and Extension," *Journal of the Society for Psychical Research*, vol. 66, no. 3, 2002.

29. G.E.R. Schwartz et al., "Accuracy and Replicability of Anomalous After-Death Communication Across Highly Skilled Mediums," *Journal of the Society for Psychical Research*, vol. 65, no. 1, 2001.

Mediums Help the Dead and the Living Connect

Suzane Northrop

When she was thirteen, Suzane Northrop communicated with her dead grandmother. While she thought it normal at the time, she soon realized other living people did not interact with the spirit world on a daily basis. So began her fame as a medium. As her skills and accuracy developed, Northrop took on more than the role of messenger. She has attempted to categorize and explain certain phenomena, and she considers herself an expert on mediums and the afterlife. In her role as expert, she has introduced phrases into the paranormal lexicon. For example, she refers to the afterlife as the Dead Person's Society *and to dead people as* DPs. *She advocates getting to know your Soul Program and Soul Self, two terms that reflect her goal of helping people negotiate a mystical journey. In this selection, from her 2002 book* Everything Happens for a Reason, *Northrop uses anecdotal evidence to show how DPs attempt to contact the living. Chance meetings and peculiar dreams are, she says, the results of deceased relatives purposefully conveying messages. She concludes that recognizing these attempts as more than coincidental or random will help our souls develop in preparation for what comes next. Northrop has authored two books, assisted police departments in solving crimes, and made numerous television and radio appearances. She is perhaps best known for taking part in* The Afterlife Experiments, *a 1999 collaboration between researchers at the Human Energy Systems Laboratory in Arizona and the cable entertainment channel HBO. In the resulting documentary, researchers tested five renowned mediums, one of which was Northrop, in controlled settings. The findings in support of an afterlife were received with popular acclaim.*

Suzane Northrop, *Everything Happens for a Reason*. Jodre Group, 2002. Copyright © 2002 by Suzane Northrop. Reproduced by permission of Northstar 2, LLC.

Several years ago a coworker and friend of mine was going through a crisis. Her stepdaughter had run away from home. My friend was devastated. She was upset all the time, and simply asking how she was doing or if she had heard anything would bring tears to her eyes.

I felt such sympathy for her. Years earlier, my sister had run away from home. My mother was a mess at the time. She was always crying and never sleeping. It went on for several months. Eventually, my sister called, but not long after that my mother developed cancer and passed on.

As I was leaving work one particular evening, I spoke to my friend and again she was in tears. She had no idea where her stepdaughter was, if she was safe, if she needed anything, or if she would ever be home.

Driving home, I turned on the radio in the car to listen to Suzane [Northrop]. It wasn't the first time I'd heard her, but as they say, timing is everything. Anyway, I listened as I drove and by the time I stopped my car I was in tears. I sat in my car for a moment and started talking to my mom. I told her about my friend at work and all that she was going through. I knew my mom would understand because of her similar circumstance. I said to her, "Mom, if what Suzane is saying is possible, then you can hear me, you know what my friend is feeling and how much pain she is in. I can't expect you to get her daughter home, but if you can just somehow relay a message to her daughter to call her mom and let her know she is safe. . . ." In my head I envisioned my mom knowing someone who knew someone who knew this young girl, and the message, the *strong* impulse to call being passed to this girl.

Anyway, I went about my evening as usual. When I got to work the next morning I was greeted by my friend, who informed me that her stepdaughter had called the night before and was safe.

Energy Is a Magnet

Souls with like energy do find one another, whether on this plane, the next, or communicating between the two. The woman in the previous story was right when she "knew" that her mother would be able to "get the message" to her friend's daughter that she ought to phone home. Souls with similar programs, similar learning tasks, or similar experiences emanate similar vibrations and "find" one another because they are pulled together by their vibratory energy. What I find is that usually in smaller groups there seems to be a coming together around a theme. In larger groups, it seems that the people that are connected by themes are drawn to sit in the same areas. Energy is a magnet. It happens in my seminars and workshops all the time, as it did when Michael and Terri attended a seminar a few years ago.

Before we talk about the last seminar we attended, there is a dream I must tell you about. Terri, my wife, was very sick one day. She dreamed that Brandon, our son, was walking by, pulling a red wagon full of babies. Terri called out, "Brandon, it's Mom." Brandon looked at her and told her, "Sorry, Mom, I am very busy right now. There's no time for you right now. I have to take care of the babies," and he continued on his way. Terri woke up and turned on the TV. All the channels were covering breaking news—the [1995] Oklahoma City bombing [of a federal office building].

When Terri and I attended our last seminar, we walked in to see people we knew, but something pulled us to sit in a different area. While Suzane was walking through the audience she stopped at our row and said, "There is a BR name," but couldn't explain further. Both my wife and the lady next to her raised their hands. Terri said, "Our son's name is Brandon." The woman next to us said her son's name was Brian. That explained the two conflicting messages. It became clear that both sons were there. Suzane looked at us and said "a large vehicle." We each explained that Brandon was killed by a school bus and Brian was killed by a tractor-trailer. Suzane continued, stating to Brian's mother, "You put large objects on the headstone." She told Suzane that they'd had an airplane put on the stone. Suzane then turned to us and said that Brandon was telling her there were a lot of things in the casket and not enough room for him. We told her we had put in his pillow and sleeping bag, some toys, his dinosnooze, and some pictures of us. After the seminar we talked to Brian's mom, shared pictures, and talked about losing our sons. We told Brian's mom about Terri's dream and she started to cry, telling us that Brian had been killed the day of the Oklahoma City bombing.

Brandon's and Brian's parents were drawn together on two levels. The fact that their children were together in spirit obviously pulled them toward one another, as did the fact that they had suffered similar losses and were both emanating similar vibratory energies. Why would Brandon's parents not have chosen to sit with the people they knew at that seminar? Simply because the "pull" of Brian's parents' vibrations was clearly much stronger than the impulse to join their friends.

Another, truly astonishing example of this occurred at a recent seminar when two couples were sitting in the same row, across the aisle from one another. Both had lost sons of the same age in car accidents, and both had second sons named Michael. It seemed that each time I received a message it applied equally to both of them. When I asked who had something in his pocket related to his son, the father of one said that he always carried a stone that would remind him of his child while the other pulled out a chain he'd given to his boy and taken from his neck after the accident that killed him. Both couples, it turned out, lived in the same city and had come to the city we were in just to attend my seminar. And, perhaps most remarkable of all, the mother of one had had an extremely vivid and detailed dream in which the other couple's son appeared. She was able to describe him precisely, even though they'd never met and at the time of the dream she had no idea who he was. As the evening progressed, it became more and more clear to me that these two families would be bonded for life because of their similar losses.

There's another example of that vibrational pull that reminded me, when I heard it, of something that might have happened in a wonderful romantic movie like *Sleepless in Seattle* or *An Affair to Remember*, in which the characters' souls—in these cases both couples were actually lovers—seemed to be drawn together by almost impossible coincidence (except, of course, that nothing is ever really *just* a coincidence). In any case, this is the story as it was reported to me by a woman who had lost both her parents and was embroiled in an extremely difficult and emotionally draining relationship with her siblings.

> The year that followed the death of my father was horrible for my relationship with my siblings. All the typical things you hear happen to families when they lose their parents—the horror stories about miscommunication and distrust that you swear could never happen in your own family—were happening in mine.
>
> The pressure was intense and I felt like (and honestly was treated like) an outsider. My siblings were each married and had children. I was not. I felt they had homes and support systems I lacked. Their primary families were still there, in their homes every day. I was alone. During the last year of my father's life I spoke to him almost every day. I saw him, at the very least, once a week. His passing left a huge void in my life, and when I turned to my family for support, I got only anger, frustration, and more problems. (To be fair, they were also recovering from a great loss, and I'm sure it was easy for each of us to see why we hurt the most and were left with the least.)
>
> Anyway, as Thanksgiving was approaching, I knew I couldn't do the "family thing." It was just too difficult and after the horrible year I'd had, the pressures were too great. I knew it

would be a recipe for disaster. My niece was spending a se-
mester in Rome, so I decided to take a ten-day tour of Italy,
including a visit with her. The trip was a gift from my dad
(from his inheritance) but became an even more important
gift.

On Thanksgiving Day I happened to be in Florence. I was
spending the afternoon on my own and decided to stop at a
café for my first taste of gelato. In line in front of me was a
man about my age, also an American. We talked for a bit
while we waited and then continued our conversation in the
square. He asked what I was doing in Florence on my own
on Thanksgiving, and I explained that my father had died
the year before and I'd just needed to get away. He said,
"The same with me, except it was my mom. I'm single and
my brothers and sisters are married, and they just don't understand what I'm going through." I said, "Same with me.
It's been horrible, and they treat me as if I'm a child and
don't have any say in anything." And he said, "Same with
me, and to make it worse my dad died almost ten years
ago." "Same with my mom," I said. And so it went.

Imagine two people going through the same thing, with the
same issues and the same reactions and the same needs,
bumping into one another in Florence while waiting in line
for gelato on Thanksgiving Day; two people who would
normally be with their families.

We spoke for a while longer and then went our separate
ways. I don't know who he is or even exactly where he's
from. We didn't exchange names or numbers. But I do know
that meeting him changed my life. I was no longer alone. I
never spoke to him again, but when things get rough with
my family I know he's out there somewhere and I'm not
alone. I was able to go home and see my family, and it
didn't hurt so much anymore when I was left out or when
they didn't call to see if I was okay, because I knew two
things—one, he was out there somewhere going through
something that is very similar, and that is somehow very

comforting. And, two, my parents were (and are) still around. They are still taking care of me and making sure I am okay. Meeting this man (although sometimes I do wonder if he was an angel) saved my spirit and was the best gift my parents could have given me.

While the vibrational pull of those suffering similar losses may be the strongest kind of bonding glue, the fact is that anyone who has suffered a loss and is trying to communicate with a loved one in spirit will be to some degree drawn to others who are doing the same. That's why when I do retreats or cruises, during which clients are, of necessity, together for an extended period of time, those events are always bonding experiences, and can also be healing simply because everyone there is more or less "in the same boat," either literally or figuratively, and they can provide solace and comfort for one another. Sometimes, in fact, I'm sure the DPs arrange it that way.

Spirits Make Simultaneous Communications

Our soul always knows where it needs to be, and because, as science has now taught us, energy exists at all points in the space-time continuum simultaneously, it's possible for the DPs to "appear to be" in more than one place at the same time—if that's what we need of them. Here's what happened when a woman came to one of my seminars in Connecticut hoping to hear from her grandma:

> The day of your seminar was a jumble and I got hopelessly lost despite stopping for directions three times. I arrived about 20 minutes late, just as you were ending your introduction and explanation of what you do. Luckily, I had gone to a workshop a few months before and had heard what I had this day missed. I wrote my gram's name, Rose, on the slip of paper and hoped.
>
> When you had everyone in the room speak about who they had seen at the gazebo [during a guided meditation] my

heart sank a little. My gram had not come to me and I thought my best chance was gone. Little did I know that two people would hear from Rose, both saying that they felt the name before the meditation (right about the time I finally got to the seminar). Rose was in the kitchen, said one lady (whom I hugged after the day was through), wearing her flowered dress and cleaning fish, which she really disliked doing. Her brother, who lived with her and is now in a convalescent home with Alzheimer's disease, used to love to fish and brought his catch home for her to clean. Oh, how she disliked it.

The woman across the room wrote down "the beach." Gram was always found in the kitchen. She never had a vacation, never traveled to the beach, never wanted to. Then it dawned on me. My mom, Gram's daughter, was at the beach this week. She was on vacation in Ocean City, Maryland. That's why she couldn't come with me that day. Gram must have gone to the beach with her. How happy that made my mom.

Grandma knew where she needed to be, to bring comfort to and acknowledge her continuing presence in the lives of both her daughter and her granddaughter. And, luckily, because God or the Higher Power has arranged it that way, she was able to be with them both. I hope she enjoyed that trip to the beach that she never got to take in life!

The same kind of simultaneous communication occurred on another occasion, when a man brought solace to both a grieving wife and a grieving daughter.

I was so excited when Suzane referred to my husband as Jimmy. I'd been to other psychics, but none of them had ever said his name. She described his favorite red and black plaid jacket and confirmed that he had died of cancer. I left her so excited, knowing that Jimmy was still with me. I was concerned that he would forget me. More importantly, while he was dying I'd been concerned that his daughter would forget him.

The next day, when I awoke, my daughter told me that she'd had a dream about her daddy the previous night. She didn't know I was at a séance with Suzane. I asked her what Daddy looked like and she said, "like Daddy." I then asked her what he was wearing in the dream. She said, "a red and black plaid jacket." I was convinced that my Jimmy had visited his daughter while Suzane brought him through. I know in my heart that he's waiting for me and that he will never forget us!

The Purpose of Separation

Earlier, I talked about the fact that families don't *necessarily* remain together after they pass—although there is always at least one loved one around to help us over, and family members are there to communicate with us when messages need to be delivered. But whether or not souls *remain* together or find one another once they've passed depends upon their individual programs.

Since no two souls have exactly the same program, DPs may or may not remain part of each other's journey in spirit. If they still have something to teach one another they will. Or they may become part of another soul's journey, as Brandon, in the story I told earlier, clearly did when he helped bring over the babies who died in Oklahoma City. Children, incidentally, also have tasks to complete, and helping other children adjust to their lives in spirit is very often one of them.

Sometimes, on the other hand, we need to stay together because our program requires it. And if that's what is required, it will happen. In fact, the lessons we have to teach one another cannot be completely learned without the use of our physical bodies from time to time; it's possible that if one soul reincarnates, the one he or she needs to be with on this plane will reincarnate as well. But that's not always possible either, because one of those souls may have some unfinished business that doesn't involve the other. And, if that's the case, we'll find another person after we reincarnate who can teach us that same lesson. It seems to me the rules get set, and just when I think they have concretized they get reset again. Ah, what an ongoing test against being rigid. Remember that it's not always one particular person we need in our life but the lesson that a certain person has to teach. There are situations, in fact, when we've been trying to resolve issues or learn a lesson from another soul and simply haven't been able to get it right, despite long and hard efforts. If that's the case, and if continuing to do the same thing over and over seems to be getting us nowhere, the gift of grace will ensure that we'll learn what we need to in some other way. The DPs want those of us they've left behind to make the choices that will help us move on, and the *Power* in charge of the "upstairs team" wants those in spirit to do the same. That's why, whatever any one soul needs to complete some unfinished aspect of its program will occur, one way or the other.

We're always drawn to one another because one of us has something to teach the other, because we both have something to learn, or because the situation created by our meeting will help our soul to grow and move on to the next level of its development. Those lessons may be as various as our programs are unique, but you can be sure there's always a reason.

Mediums Are Part of the Spiritualist Religion

John Walliss

Spiritualism is the religion that has arisen around the idea that the living can communicate with the dead. Mediums, therefore, are central components of Spiritualism. In this excerpt, John Walliss reports his findings regarding mediums and Spiritualism. He explains that spirits communicate in order to achieve precise goals: to give advice, to offer support, to prove they exist, and to send "healing energies." These goals fall under the more general terms of information sharing and negotiation. Walliss also debates whether or not Spiritualism's Seven Principles allow for mediums and their messages. Many believe that principle #3, "The Communion of Saints and the Ministry of Angels," refers to the communication between mediums and spirits. Walliss concludes that Spiritualism provides a unique way for the living to continue having a meaningful relationship with those who have passed on, but the presence of mediums within the religion is not a major draw for newcomers.

John Walliss has a PhD from the University of Sheffield in the United Kingdom. He is a lecturer in sociology at Liverpool Hope University in England and has written widely on religion and sociology.

The 'birth' of modern Spiritualism is typically dated as 31 March 1848 when percussive raps were heard in the vicinity of two teenage sisters, Kate and Margaret Fox, living in Hydesville, New York. Over time the sisters devised a code whereby questions could be asked and answers allegedly received from a spirit calling himself Charles B. Rosna (Carroll,

John Walliss, "Continuing Bonds: Relationships Between the Living and the Dead Within Contemporary Spiritualism," *Mortality*, v. 6, 2001. Reproduced by permission of Taylor & Francis, Ltd. and the author.

1997). The publicity generated by this led to an upsurge in public interest in the possibility of spiritual communication to the extent that

> By 1850—only two years after the Hydesville happenings—it was estimated that there were a hundred mediums in New York City, and fifty or sixty 'private circles' in Philadelphia. A decade later, believers could be numbered in their millions (Brandon, 1983: 42).

The growth of Spiritualism in the [United Kingdom], however, proceeded much more slowly. Whilst there were mediums already working in public, it was not until after the publicity generated by the visit from the USA in 1852 of two mediums, Mrs. Hayden and Mrs. Roberts, that Spiritualism became absorbed, with other phenomena such as phrenology and mesmerism, into the wider religious and philosophical debate about the meaning of existence. Davies (1999), for example, notes two broad responses within Christianity to Spiritualism during this period. On the one hand, some saw it as an unwelcome return of pre-Enlightenment superstition and, in some instances, representing a technique whereby Satan and demonic forces could be channelled. However, others ". . . from across the religious spectrum embraced spiritualism as an invigorating affirmation of Christian doctrine on life after death, and also, as with mesmerism, saw in it a potential avenue of spiritual healing" (Davies, 1999: 31).[1] Moreover, the phenomenon of 'table-turning' and 'spirit rapping' became for a section of the population a pass-time; "it was not long before 'table turning' became socially acceptable. Smart ladies served tea and then retired to 'communicate' with the spirit. For them it was a social pass-time. But there were others for whom 'Spiritualism' became a way of life" (Bassett, 1990: 9). For these individuals, who joined together to form the Spiritualist National Union (SNU) in 1890, Spiritualism offered "a Religion of Reason for all those who see this as an Age of Reason" (Meynell, 1998: no pagination).

Mediums and the World Wars

However, it was during and after the Great War [World War I] that Spiritualism grew rapidly, both in influence and membership. As Hazelgrove (2000; see also Winter, 1995: 54–77) has recently noted, during this period large numbers of people who had lost loved ones on the front line flocked to mediums to receive messages from them and to maintain a form of relationship with them.[2] In this way, "mediums performed . . . therapeutic services for the bereaved" whilst "Spiritualism acted as a kind of living memorial to the dead" (Hazelgrove, 2000: 35). This, however, alongside the numbers of fraudulent mediums charging large fees for final messages from loved ones, led to a backlash against the movement (see Bassett, 1990: 33). *The Umpire*, for example, spoke out in August 1916 against what it saw as the "harpies of humanity trading upon the mental crucifixion of those whose loved ones have fallen to die upon the wasted fields of France and Flanders" (Bassett, 1990: 34). Likewise, Elliot O'Donnell wrote in his 1920 book *The Menace of Spiritualism* of how

> The war has made people so anxious to glean tidings of another world that they will jump at anything, however remote and trivial . . . and of this the mediums are thoroughly well aware. They know they have only to weave even the barest semblance of truth into one of their messages, and their poor, half-demented clients will joyfully accept all that follows, convinced that it is of spirit origin (O'Donnell, 1920: 158).

It was the Second World War, however, that represented Spiritualism's 'finest hour' (Akhtar & Humphries, 1999), although in many ways it was a bitter-sweet time. As during the Great War, Spiritualist mediums came under attack from the authorities who feared, for example, that Nazi spies might infiltrate séances to obtain war secrets from dead naval men (Hazelgrove, 2000). The medium, Helen Duncan, for example was convicted in 1944 at the Old Bailey under the 1735 Witchcraft Act after she had allegedly informed a woman at a séance of the sinking of her son's ship and his death three weeks before the sinking was officially announced. However, despite this, according to *Psychic News* the number of Spiritualists quadrupled from around 250,000 in the 1930s to one million in 1944.[3] Again, many of these were seeking messages from loved ones killed in battle or, in some cases, predictions of forthcoming air attacks. Indeed, as Akhtar and Humphries (1999: 72) note, "assurances to those that attended [spiritualist churches] that they would come to no harm in the attacks seems to have given many renewed strength and confidence to carry on".

Spiritualism in Decline

In the decades following the war, however, both the number of Spiritualists and the influence of Spiritualism has declined. At the end of 1997, for example, the Spiritualist National Union (SNU) had 381 affiliated churches, with a total membership of 20,026.[4] Whilst, in many ways this decline may be understood within the context of wider patterns showing a decline in religious attendance in the UK in the post-war period generally (see Davie, 1994: 45–73), a number of authors have suggested factors implicit within Spiritualism itself for the decline in its fortunes. Akhtar and Humphries (1999), for example, argue that for the baby-boom generation onwards Spiritualism seemed too 'cosy', personal, family-oriented and, in particular, associated with the older generation. Similarly, Spencer (2001) argues that "it seems difficult to imagine that the public association of mediums with fraud enhanced spiritualism's attractiveness to the uncommitted or potential converts". Linked to this, as previously noted, Spiritualism's greatest growth periods during the last century were during the mass-bereavement of the two World Wars. On this basis, it could be argued that the last 50 years of, on the whole, peacetime within the West is not conducive to a mass interest in

Spiritualist phenomenon. Rather, the bereavements that potentially lead to an involvement in Spiritualism are more than likely to be those of, relatively speaking, isolated individuals. Indeed, it is highly possible that the 'privatisation' of death and bereavement could be a factor in this, with the bereaved either wishing to 'detach and move on' or to continue bonds privately or in a non-religious context.

Spiritualism's Principles Include Mediums

Whilst Spiritualism has no set creed or dogma, it does possess a philosophy, known as *The Seven Principles*, although individual Spiritualists often display a high degree of reflexivity in their interpretation of them;[5]

1. The Fatherhood of God
2. The Brotherhood of Man
3. The Communion of Saints and the Ministry of Angels
4. Continuous Existence of the Human Soul
5. Personal Responsibility
6. Compensation and Retribution hereafter for all the Good and Evil Deeds done on Earth
7. Eternal Progress open to Every Human SoulWhilst all are interlinked and of equal importance for the religion of Spiritualism, for our purposes here it is only necessary to pull out one of these *Principles* in depth; 'The Communion of Saints and the Ministry of Angels'. To quote from an introductory leaflet produced by the SNU on Spiritualism,[6] this belief "is the key around which our whole philosophy turns". Thus, whereas 'Orthodoxy' denies the possibility of such a relationship, believing often that physical death represents the end of an individual's existence, ". . . for the past one hundred and twenty years we have proved conclusively that man [*sic*] not only survives physical death but is able, through mediums, to communicate with those left be-

hind". Indeed, "not only that, they spend quite a lot of time giving us help and guidance in various ways with our earthly problems".

This 'proof of survival' is provided within Spiritualism, then, largely through the 'demonstration' of mediumship, which is a prominent feature of Spiritualist services. This is the, typically half-hour, segment in which the medium communicates messages from those in the Spirit World to the congregation (see Martin, 1970: 152–155). In the following section I intend to describe the nature of this continuing relationship between the living and the deceased through an examination of the different elements or strands that may be found within these messages. . . .

Why Spirits Communicate Through Mediums

The demonstration of mediumship may be usefully envisaged as a three-way relationship between three social actors, only two of whom are empirically present,[7] characterized by *information sharing* and *negotiation*; The role of the medium in the demonstration is, as the name suggests, to act as an intermediary between the worlds. This can take one of two forms. In the first, the medium is *passive* and is possessed by the particular spirit for whom (s)he becomes an 'instrument'. In this condition, the spirit manifests through the medium who adopts, for example, the mannerisms, posture and in some instances the voice and/or facial characteristics of the deceased. This 'physical' form of mediumship is relatively rare today, having seemingly been superseded by more 'mental' or psychological form.[8] In these the medium acts as an *active* intermediary between the living and the deceased by gathering super-sensory information from the spirit, translating and selecting from this and then presenting their interpretation to the congregation in the hope that someone will be able to 'take' the message (see Skultans, 1974).[9]

In other instances, however, the medium may come straight to a particular member of the congregation with a name or a description:

> Can I come to you my love please with the green jacket on? . . . Speak up because I want to come to you my love because I've got a lady by the name of Elsie that was calling through and I've got another lady but I don't know which is which at the moment.

The message is then 'verbally negotiated' (Wooffitt, 2000) by the medium and a specific member of the congregation with the latter giving clarification through 'yes' or 'no' responses, gathering and interpreting the evidence given by the medium and then giving either positive ('that's Aunt Jane') or negative ('I don't know anybody fitting that description') feedback.[10] This process is then repeated typically until the individual can 'take' the spirit and their message, although in some instances it can continue throughout the message albeit interspersed with the other elements that I shall discuss below. It can also sometimes transpire, and has always been the case when I have personally received one, that a message cannot be accepted on either factual grounds or because the spirit cannot be recognised. This could potentially call into question the charisma of the individual medium—but not, interestingly, the process itself (Wooffitt, 2000). As a result, mediums typically do one of two things. Usually, the reluctant recipient is asked to 'go away and think about it'; to, for example, ask older relatives whether they remember the person attempting to communicate, or, in the case of factual information, to go away and mull the information over. Alternatively, the medium may explicitly open the message up to the rest of the congregation by saying 'can anyone else accept this message?'. Where there is an acceptance, and there invariably is, the process will continue.

Messages to the Living

The evidence given for survival may also, aside from just information, inherently contain important messages to the living. For example, part of the message could be the spirit telling the congregation member that they're 'OK' and that they're settling into their new existence. Linked to this, (s)he may also want to let them know that, for example, their death was peaceful, that they were aware of their love and help towards the end of life (this is often the case with those who were not lucid towards the end) or that any ailments that they suffered from in life are now absent. In addition, (s)he may also speak of family and friends who had 'passed over' beforehand with whom they have met up again. Indeed, it is often the case that mediums can relay a set of messages to an individual from a number of spirits, a phenomenon that may be likened to, for example, the image of relatives passing around the telephone receiver on a special occasion.

Proof of survival and some information about their passing and present condition, then, is a key aspect of the messages delivered through mediums. The other dominant theme in the messages may be expressed as '*I'm still here for* (or *with*) *you and ...*'. In other words, the spirit will affirm their continued interest in, and relationship with, the living and seek to assist in a number of ways. . . . Whilst, as will be discussed below, these ways are often inter-related, in general terms two general strands within the messages may be discerned: *advice* and *support*.

Mediums Translate Advice from Spirits

In the first instance, the deceased may wish to offer advice to the individual. This may be at the general level and include relatively mundane advice such as the location of misplaced objects, how to deal with unruly children or even gardening and home improvement. In other instances advice is offered concerning life plans:

> But I feel on the material pathway my love [that] we're coming to a crossroads where we have to make a decision ... And I feel that there again nobody can tell us what to do or how to go about it but I feel very strongly that if we simply relax and we learn to tune into our spiritual selves we instinctively *know* the right direction to travel in ...

In some cases the deceased may offer warnings or attempt to raise the individual's awareness of a particular (possibly dangerous) situation or relationship. One woman, for example, was alerted to problems within her marriage through messages over a period of time as well as through her own clairvoyance. However, the majority of those whom I spoke to were uneasy about whether such messages should be seen as explicit warnings or, more specifically, a form of prophecy, for two main reasons. Firstly, for many it contradicts the ideas of free-will and personal responsibility inherent within the *Seven Principles* by effectively handing over one's destiny to another. ...

The second reason is historical and relates to the fact that, as noted previously, a medium could be prosecuted for prophecy until relatively recently (1951) under the Witchcraft Act. As a result, contemporary mediums are keen to distance themselves from this phenomenon. Moreover, Spiritualists are also arguably aware of the disillusionment that was generated within the movement before and during the Second World War as a result of a number of incorrect predictions (Nelson, 1969).[11] Nevertheless, prophecy of a kind does continue albeit in a more subtle form by the medium raising the individual's awareness of a particular issue, e.g. 'there's going to be a new life around you'. Similarly, they may shift a message into a prophecy. This phenomenon was picked up by one Spiritualist that I interviewed:

> So, if a person can't take the message [the medium will] say 'have you lost a purse?' and [the member of the congregation will] say 'no'. They'll say 'well, be careful because you might do [so]'.

Those I spoke to, however, were much less reticent about receiving advice regarding their spiritual development from the deceased or spirit guides. Indeed, a number said how such communications were often the catalyst for them beginning to develop spiritually or develop as mediums and/or healers. . . .

A final form of advice that is sometimes found within Spiritual communication regards family members, particularly partners, 'letting go' of their deceased loved ones and 'moving on'. At one of the first services that I attended, for example, one gentleman was told that he had grieved for 'too long' for his wife and that—while keeping her in his thoughts—he had to stop obsessively grieving for her. . . .

The Dead Can Offer Support to the Living

The deceased may also wish to offer support or emotional assistance to their loved ones. Indeed, in many ways support is intrinsically bound up with the advice given. . . . Moreover, because the support is typically non-directive those I spoke to felt much more comfortable about accepting it than they did when advice was given.

There were, however, reservations in some instances. This was particularly the case in messages of reconciliation, where the deceased wishes to say either what was not said or what they perhaps felt that they could not say whilst they were alive. To give an excerpt from a lengthy message of this kind:

> Would you understand why this gentleman wants to particularly talk to his son? Because there's something, either words were said or there was some uneasiness, something was unresolved when he went to the Spirit World and you're able to pass this on are you? Because he really needs to do this because as this gentleman is coming in here *he is so sorry*. . . . And I know here that he is so sorry, maybe not for what has happened but I feel here that this bridge needs to be built and he needs to know there's nothing, there's no malice, there's no unnecessary hurt or anything like that. . . .

Thus, the deceased will seek to repair the relationship with the living by expressing regret and asking them, as in this example, to put the past behind them. Similarly, as in this next example, they may also wish to express to the individual(s) concerned what they perhaps couldn't say whilst they were alive:

> He'd try and do his best ... I feel as if he tried and he wants to emphasise that because I feel as if I wanted to try. Not everything worked out and not everything I would have wanted happened but in his own way he wants to get across 'I tried'. Would you understand that, please?...

Those that received such messages, however, typically expressed an ambivalence towards them. One man, for example, told me that although such messages helped him to grow and "get [that person's] life and that relationship into much more perspective", he felt that it was "a bit ironic that the communications that have achieved the reconciliation come after life rather than during life ... I'd have liked that communication if only it could have taken place beforehand". Similarly, another expressed an uneasiness at the idea that an individual could "really mess someone's life up while they were alive and then come back and say 'I'm sorry' and everything was all right".

Healing Energies

The final sense in which the deceased may wish to assist the living is by sending them 'healing energies'. This is typically done in one of two ways. Primarily, it may be stated explicitly by the medium, for instance, saying to the congregation member that 'this individual also wants to send you their healing thoughts' or 'I know that she's sending you her healing energies'. In other cases elements of the evidence for survival may become metaphors for healing or support. Thus, in this example the deceased's walking stick which had been used previously as a piece of evidence becomes a metaphor for emotional support:

And I know he had a stick towards the end of his life ...
Well, he's just showing me a stick here and he's saying 'I
needed that for support' and I know he wants to give that
for you, not in a physical way, but emotionally here where
you need a bit of support at the moment and he's saying
'I'm here for you, very much here for you' ... I want to give
you this walking stick so that when you're just feeling a bit
low, you know it's there for you.

The Role of the Deceased in Spiritualism

At first glance, then, it could be argued that in many ways
within Spiritualism the deceased occupy a dominant position.
Thus, the emphasis is placed on what they can do for the living—typically offer advice and support—not *vice versa*. They
are not, for example, dependent on the prayers of the living to
assist them through Purgatory. Moreover, as Spiritualists are
keen to point out, during the demonstration of mediumship
it is those in the Spirit World rather than the living who
choose who gets a message and from whom. To quote one
medium I spoke to, "Spirit goes where the message is needed
the most ... Spirits know more than we do and they guide
you to go to that person that really needs a message". However, this is not to say that the living exercise no authority. As
I have already noted, where they do recognise the communicator and remember the advice given this does not mean that
they will act on it.

In this way, the relationship between the 'worlds' does not
fit comfortably into the broad typology of possible relationships with the dead recently proposed by Klass and Goss
(1999). In comparison, for example, with the ancestral relationships of Japan, the Spiritualist dead are not treated with
any level of veneration or worship. They may of course be ad-
mired or adored, but this attitude of the living is usually a
secular rather than a spiritual affair; admiring them for their
success in life or character rather than because of their role as
an ancestor. Equally, there is no sense of 'mutual obligations'

between the 'worlds' or that the inhabitants of both have "equal power to help and hurt" (Klass & Goss, 1999: 548). The living, for example, are not expected to perform rituals for the dead, as in Japanese ancestor worship, or envisaged as having any power to assist the deceased in any way. Similarly, the deceased cannot help in any other sense than perhaps through the relatively indirect ways that I have discussed above. There is also most definitely no way in which they may be perceived to 'hurt' the living except, again at the indirect level, by their apparent inability or unwillingness to communicate via a medium to their loved ones.

The deceased are therefore also not seen as having become the 'sacred dead' and thus having attained any special insights or powers following their death. For example, they are never seen as having the ability to intercede with the Supreme Being on behalf of the living. Moreover, their insights into life are not seen as those of 'ascended masters' nor is their advice coloured by a form of post-mortem objectivity (see Nelson, 1969: 28–29). Rather they are typically seen to be the same as they were whilst alive and are therefore not treated with any form of reverence:

> Just because they're in Spirit, they're actually just the same ... and if they were completely stupid and missed the point while they were alive they might not be that different now. And if when they were alive you never took their advice then y'know ... just because our spirit relatives come back doesn't mean that they suddenly become these wonderful growthful spiritual beings, because whilst that might be a purpose for them they might not have got that far and they might just be coming back in a different form but really as much as they were before.

In this way I would argue that the relationship is typically seen to represent a *literal continuation* of the relationship that occurred during life (see Young & Cullen, 1996: 173–174). Thus, someone who was 'completely stupid and missed the point' whilst alive will similarly be more than likely the last person that advice would be sought or accepted from now they are dead. Likewise, referring back to a previous point, someone with whom one had a negative experience in life—a parent, for example—will generally not be treated with any more civility than they would have received whilst alive nor will they be instantly forgiven for what potentially occurred in life. Indeed, the phenomenon of 'forgiving the dead' is perhaps the only way in which the dead are dependent on the living and the only 'service' that the living may provide. . . .

Spiritualism Lets Our Relationships Continue

To conclude, Spiritualism may be seen to offer a means and a supportive environment where a type of relationship can continue between those on both sides of the 'Great Divide'. This relationship is in many ways a continuation of the lived one, with the deceased offering support and advice which the living can then either act on or not. Indeed, in many cases it is not so much the content of the communications *per se* that is significant for people, but rather the fact that their loved ones have communicated with them. However, it would be wrong to claim that those involved in Spiritualism are solely motivated by a desire for such communication. . . . Whilst bereavement may be a factor leading to involvement, it is not on the whole a significant one. Moreover, the desire to maintain communication with the deceased is not in itself a significant factor in why individuals continue to attend Spiritualist services. Rather, it is their relationship with others in the congregation and an interest in the philosophy of Spiritualism that tends to maintain individuals' involvement. In other words, whilst the phenomenon of spirit communication is an intrinsic part of Spiritualism—enshrined as it is in the *Seven Principles*—it would be wrong to see it as its sole *raison d'être*. There are, however, sites at which I feel that this would be the case. Primarily, at public demonstrations of mediumship that take place outside of the context of religious worship—in, for example, clubs and pubs—and where individuals who are not necessarily Spiritualists have private sittings with mediums. At these I believe there would be an emphasis on the *phenomenon* of Spiritualism—in particular, spirit communication—and its value as a form of entertainment above and beyond any, strictly speaking, religious concerns. Further research, however, would be needed to examine whether or not this is the case.

Notes

1. For further discussions of the origins of modern British Spiritualism, see Barrow (1986), Hallam *et al.* (1999) and Howarth (2000).

2. This included a number of 'high profile conversions'. Sir Arthur Conan Doyle and his wife became involved in Spiritualism in 1917, becoming the chairman of several Spiritualist institutions and a tireless propagandist for it until his death in 1930 (see Conan Doyle, 1997). Likewise, the editor of *The People*, Hannen Swaffer, became a Spiritualist in 1925 and regular feature writer in *Psychic Times* after becoming convinced that he had received messages from his former boss, the newspaper tycoon, Lord Northcliffe. Other famous 'converts' included Sir Oliver Lodge and the socialist writer, Robert Blatchford (see Akhtar & Humphries, 1999: 71; Bassett, 1990: 34; Hazelgrove, 2000: 15–16).

3. This figure is arguably an exaggeration. According to official figures, the number of SNU societies and members was actually *falling* during this period. This figure may, however, include members of private circles or other Spiritualist Associations who were not necessarily members of the SNU. See note 5 below. If one accepts the official SNU figure, then the number of SNU members has generally grown over the course of the century. I have no figures for the number of Spiritualist churches during the twentieth century as a whole, although—again drawing on Nelson's (1969: 286) figures—the number of churches has decreased in the post-war period from 400 to 381 in 1997.

4. In addition there were another 2007 Class B members and 352 provisional Class B members (source: SNU website: http://www.snu.org.uk/members.htm). There are, of course, no figures for those who attend Spiritualist churches or centres and who do not become members of the SNU. It should also be remembered that a number of individuals are not members of the SNU for a variety of reasons, but would still see themselves as being Spiritualists. For a review of SNU statistics between 1908 and 1964 see Nelson (1969: 273–288).

5. 'With liberty of interpretation' is a common phrase used within Spiritualism when discussing the *Principles*. For example, in the 1976 edition of the SNU Hymn Book this phrase is presented in italics below the list of *Principles* on the first page. Likewise in the *Principles of Spiritualism* leaflet (see below), the reader is reminded that "it should be borne in mind that these are principles, not commandments, and in accepting them, one is accorded complete liberty of interpretation". Whilst this phrase was legally removed from the aforementioned hymn book in

its following edition, the idea is still implicit within the religion. This reflexivity in interpretation was also a persistent theme in interviews and my discussions with Spiritualists.

6. The leaflet entitled *For Those New to Spiritualism, 2. The Principles of Spiritualism* was purchased from the Chesterfield SNU centre.

7. For the purpose of this paper I intend to 'bracket out' the question of whether the spiritual communications emanate from a supernatural source or whether mediumship is a form of trickery. There is a wealth of literature for both positions (see Bjorling, 1998). Rather, my account will be phenomenological and will seek to describe the phenomenon as it is understood and articulated by those present. Thus, I will speak of 'the deceased' because that is whom those whom I spoke to believe they are receiving communications from via mediums and because, ultimately, I can make no judgements of the ontological existence, or not, of spirits.

8. Mental mediumship falls into three broad categories; *Clairvoyance* (the medium sees the spirit); *Clairaudience* (the medium hears the spirit) and *Clairsentience* (the medium senses the presence and the thoughts of the spirit). (Source: SNU website: http://www.snu.org.uk/index2.htm).

9. One medium that I have seen demonstrate on many occasions during the period of my fieldwork consistently 'sees' deep pink roses which she then interprets to the congregation member with, for example, a small white bud symbolising a deceased infant or the thorns on the stem representing life's woes. The spiritual roses are then given symbolically to the particular individual at the end of the message.

10. An in-depth discussion of this process is outside of the scope of this paper; see, however, Martin (1970) and Wooffitt (2000).

11. For example, two weeks before the outbreak of the war, *Two Worlds* ran a headline declaring that there would be 'No World War'. A number of other predictions, ultimately incorrect, were also made such as that the war would only last three years, that Italy would remain neutral and that Hitler would die of throat cancer before 1942 (see Nelson, 1969: 162–163).

References

1. M. Akhtar & S. Humphries (1999), *Far out: the dawning of New Age Britain*. Bristol: Sansom & Company Ltd.

2. L. Barrow (1986), *Independent spirits: Spiritualism and English plebeians 1850–1910*. London: Routledge.

3. J. Bassett (1990), *100 years of national Spiritualism*. London: Spiritualists National Union.

4. J. Bjorling (1998), *Consulting spirits: a bibliography*. Westport, CT: Greenwood Press.

5. J. Bowlby (1971), *Attachment & loss: vol. 1. Attachment*. Harmondsworth, UK: Pelican Books.

6. R. Brandon (1983), *The Spiritualists: the passion for the occult in the nineteenth and twentieth century*. London: Weidenfeld & Nicolson.

7. B.E. Carroll (1997), *Spiritualism in antebellum America*. Bloomington: Indiana University Press.

8. A. Conan Doyle (1997), *Full report of a lecture on Spiritualism delivered by Sir Arthur Conan Doyle*. Cambridge, UK: Rupert Books.

9. G. Davie (1994), *Religion in Britain since 1945: believing without belonging.* Oxford: Blackwell.

10. O. Davies (1999), *Witchcraft, magic and culture 1736–1951.* Manchester, UK: Manchester University Press.

11. E. Hallam, J. Hockey & G. Howarth (1999), *Beyond the body: death and social identity.* London: Routledge.

12. J. Hazelgrove (2000), *Spiritualism and British society between the wars.* Manchester, UK: Manchester University Press.

13. G. Howarth (2000), "Dismantling the boundaries between life and death," *Mortality, 5* (2), 127–138.

14. D. Klass & R. Goss (1999), "Spiritual bonds to the dead in cross-cultural and historical perspective: comparative religion and modern grief," *Death Studies, 23,* 347–367.

15. B. Martin (1970), "The Spiritualist meeting," *A Sociological Yearbook of Religion, 3,* 146–161.

16. K. Meynell (1998), *What is Spiritualism?* http://www.snu.org.uk/spirit.html

17. G. Nelson (1969), *Spiritualism and society.* London: Routledge & Kegan Paul.

18. E. O'Donnell (1920), *The menace of Spiritualism.* London: Werner & Laurie.

19. V. Skultans (1974), *Intimacy and ritual: a study of Spiritualism, mediums and groups.* London: Routledge & Kegan Paul.

20. W. Spencer (2001), "To absent friends: Spiritualist mediumship and New Age channeling compared and contrasted," *Journal of Contemporary Religion,* in press.

21. J. Winter (1995), *Sites of memory, sites of mourning: the Great War in European cultural history.* Cambridge, UK: Cambridge University Press.

22. R. Wooffitt (2000), "Some properties of the interactional organisation of displays of paranormal cognition in psychic-sitter interaction," *Sociology, 34* (3), 457–479.

23. M. Young & L. Cullen (1996), *A good death (conversations with east Londoners).* London: Routledge.

Mediums Have Passed Scientific Tests

Gary E. Schwartz

This excerpt is one of the concluding chapters to Gary E. Schwartz's book The Afterlife Experiments, *a popular first-person account of experiments involving five mediums: Laurie Campbell, John Edward, Suzane Northrop, Anne Gehman, and George Anderson. The experiments took place in 1999 and were filmed by the cable entertainment network HBO.*

Schwartz is a borderline skeptic who wants to believe, but only if science can be the support. In pursuing this goal, he has become very familiar with common skeptical claims. In this excerpt he lists eleven ways that skeptics try to undermine mediums. Then, going point by point, Schwartz explains what the skeptics say, what the mediums say, and what his experiments revealed.

Schwartz is the director of the Human Energy Systems Laboratory in Tucson, Arizona. He is a professor of clinical psychology at the University of Arizona.

On January 1, 2000, [my colleague] Linda [Russek] and I made an unusual New Year's resolution, or more precisely, a New Millennium resolution.

We decided we would try to live our lives as if the living soul hypothesis [which states that the soul survives in the afterlife] were true, so long as there was no convincing data to the contrary. From that day forward, so long as the survival hypothesis was plausible, we would attempt to make personal decisions with the awareness that our lives might continue after we physically died. We would live our personal lives as a great experiment.

If our decision is mistaken, and the truth is really ashes to ashes, dust to dust, we will never know that the experiment failed.

However, if our assumption is correct and the living soul is a doorway into the existence of a larger reality, a living spiritual/energy reality, then when we die, we will be aware that our consciousness continues. And we will be relieved to discover that the choices we made were wise ones.

One of the members of our anonymous Friendly Devil's Advocates committee informed us that this same decision was arrived at many years ago by the great seventeenth-century mathematician Blaise Pascal. We reasoned that if the logic was good enough for Pascal, it should make sense for us, as well.

There's also another reason for conducting our lives as if the living soul hypothesis is true. This, too, comes from the canons of science in the form of a principle known as Occam's razor, after the thirteenth-century English philosopher who first enunciated the idea. One way of stating his principle is this: "All things being equal, the simpler hypothesis is usually the correct one."

Here's a favorite example of the wisdom of this simple statement. When stargazers of the Middle Ages went about gathering the evidence being revealed to them by the newly invented telescope, the earth-centered model of the universe became ever more complicated as the observers tried to account for the ever more contradictory data. One advantage of the new but highly controversial sun-centered model that landed Galileo in so much hot water was just that it was *simpler* in the sense that it could account for more of the data. One idea could account for so many observations—the idea, in a word, was elegant.

The same logic applies to the emerging data unfolding not only in our experiments, but in the history of mediumship research over the past hundred years. As described in Alan Gauld's book *Mediumship and Survival*, a definitive history of a century of investigations addressing the living soul hypothesis, the number of different explanations needed to account for all the data is itself extraordinary. The best experiments on this subject can be explained away only if one makes a whole series of assumptions:

- Some of the findings would require that mediums were secretly using detectives who were so good as to be themselves undetected by other detectives—"super cheating."

- Some of the findings would require that the sitters were falsely remembering specific facts of their personal histories, including relatives' names and causes of death—"super sitter bias."

- Some of the findings would require that the mediums were extraordinary guessers of information, even when the sitters were not saying a word and the mediums could not see them—"super guessing."

- Some of the findings would require that the mediums were interpreting subtle changes in the sitter's breathing so as to figure out, for example, that the sitter's grandmother had brought daisies to her mother's wedding—"super subtle cue reading."

- Some of the findings would require that the mediums were reading not only the unconscious mind of the sitters, but information that the sitters themselves could not remember or remembered wrong, only later to verify it through a conversation with another relative—"super telepathy."

However, if we were to apply Occam's razor to the total set of data collected over the past hundred years, . . . there is a straightforward hypothesis that is elegant in its simplicity.

This is the simple hypothesis that consciousness continues after death. This hypothesis accounts for all the data.

If we are to take the process of science seriously, there comes a point when it makes sense to accept the principle of Occam's razor: sometimes the simpler hypothesis is the correct one.

And sometimes it is the tiniest piece of data that reminds us of this simple truth.

John Edward Convinces Schwartz

If there is any one single piece of mediumship data that led me to accept the living soul hypothesis, it is a brief and seemingly silly incident that occurred in a John Edward reading on television.

He was speaking with a woman who appeared to be in her early thirties and was receiving information about one of her older deceased relatives. He then said something like "She is showing me a little dog. Did your relative have a little dog?"

The woman looked confused. She did not know whether her relative had a little dog or not.

Then John said something that truly surprised me. He said, "She's telling me that the dog was named after a food. A food name."

A food name for a dog? What could it possibly be? Lettuce? Banana? Hamburger? Here, little Carrot. Roll over, Grits. Tortilla, play dead!

Not likely.

After the reading, the sitter was then shown calling her aunt to ask about the deceased relative's dog. The relative had, indeed, owned a little dog. When the sitter asked for its name, the relative replied, "Popsicles."

That sounded almost as weird as Grits or Tortilla. The sitter asked her aunt about the strange name, and she replied, "Because the dog loved popsicles."

Being the enthusiastic agnostic that I am, I ticked off the skeptical possibilities about detectives ... or some deceit off camera to make it look as if John had done something remarkable when he was really cheating ... or reading the mind of the audience member ... or an amazing guess ...

Or was this just another innocent and tiny little piece of data suggesting that John really does talk to dead people?

What do you think?

Here's what I think, as a scientist.

The probability that John is the real thing—and that Laurie [Campbell], Suzane [Northrop] Anne [Gehman] George [Anderson], and certain other mediums are engaged in something honest and truly spiritual—is as great as the probability that the light from distance stars continues in some form, forever.

And I remember what Professor [and philosopher] William James wrote about Mrs. Piper, a medium he studied very carefully:

> I should be willing now to stake as much money on Mrs. Piper's honesty as on that of anyone I know, and I am quite satisfied to leave my reputation for wisdom or folly, so far as human nature is concerned, to stand or fall by this declaration.

Reviewing the Data

... I can no longer ignore the data and dismiss the words. They are as real as the sun, the trees, and our television sets, which seem to pull pictures out of the air.

So what do I recommend?

That we celebrate the Big H, memorable moments on the beach, the "Good Ship Lollipop," the cow in the backyard, and daisies at the wedding.

That we celebrate the billions of trillions of stars and the physical miracle that their light shines forever.

That we celebrate the existence of the human mind, which not only raises scientific questions but also evolves the wisdom to know when it's time to stop obsessively questioning and accept the truth of the answers.

That we celebrate the existence of living souls in a living and evolving universe.

And that, with humility, we thank a Loving Essence that makes all of this possible.

The Eleven Key Summary Points

1. Fraud
2. Cueing
3. Selective memory
4. Vague information
5. Lucky guesses
6. Experimenter bias or mistakes
7. Motivation of the mediums
8. Motivation of the skeptics
9. Mind-reading by mediums
10. Memory in the universe
11. Talking to dead people

In the following analysis, it's important to understand that we are not analyzing the work of *all* mediums. Many mediums—perhaps even *most* mediums—are giving their clients what the clients want, very much in the same way people go to a magic show to have the magician dazzle and please them. The principal difference is that the paying customer at the magic show knows that trickery is being used, and the paying customer in the medium's living room wants to believe.

No, it's not the psychic medium using cold reading techniques we're evaluating here, but only the small, highly select group of top mediums who have been willing to risk exposure and humiliation by allowing scientific examination of their work under highly controlled circumstances.

So here's what the data show about the experiments involving this small group of mediums:

Point 1: Fraud

Skeptics Speculate: They somehow get information ahead of time, by detectives or other secret means.

Mediums Say: We do not know who the sitters are, not only in the laboratory studies but also in our daily practices.

What the Experiments Actually Reveal: In parts of the experiments, the mediums could indeed have cheated by having taps placed on the lab's phones and our home phones so they could obtain the names of all the sitters in advance, then scouting or hiring a detective to get useful information, and memorizing all the information.

But this would not have helped for the silent periods in [one set of] experiments because the mediums could not see who was sitting behind them or on the other side of the screen. And they could not know the order in which the sitters would be brought to them (which was decided only at the last minute, on the day of the testing). Since the sitter did not speak during the silent period, the medium had no clues to age, sex, emotional state, or anything else that would have been revealed by seeing or hearing the sitter.

What's more, in [one particular] experiment, the sitters were not even in the same location as the medium, and the most impressive data were provided even before any telephone contact was established.

Point 2: Cueing

Skeptics Speculate: The mediums get information by studying facial expressions and non-verbal cues, analyzing the verbal content, interpreting tone of voice, and using other tricks of cold reading.

Mediums Say: We do not need to see the sitters, or even hear their voices, to get accurate information, and the experiments were successful even when we could not see the sitters and they did not speak.

What the Experiments Actually Reveal: In [one set of] experiments, the mediums were deaf and blind to the sitters. Yet, in the absence of any verbal or visual cues, they still provided a very large amount of data, of which 40 percent to 80 percent was scored as +3, absolutely accurate. In the HBO study, one medium in particular, Suzane Northrop, asked only five questions but reported more than 120 pieces of information that were rated over 80 percent accurate. Again, in [another] experiment, the barriers between medium and sitters were even more distinct, yet the medium's accuracy was astonishing.

Point 3: Selective Memory

Skeptics Speculate: The sitters primarily remember the hits and forget the misses because they're grieving and want to believe. This inflates their remembered accuracy, creating a self-fulfilling illusion that is completely false.

Mediums Say: Except for information that seems sensitive and should be kept private, we convey everything we receive. Our clients mostly remember the hits because there are so many of them.

What the Experiments Actually Reveal: The scoring techniques used in the laboratory in these experiments did not rely on the sitters' overall memories of the readings but were scored from the transcripts of what the mediums actually said. The sitters carefully scored every piece of data; when the medium said something like "the number six, which could mean the month of June or the sixth of a month," the sitter would score each of the statements, likely scoring one of the items as a hit and the other as a miss. Data evaluated this way, and showing high rates of accuracy, cannot be explained by selective remembering.

Point 4: Vague Information

Skeptics Speculate: The information mediums claim to receive is so vague and general that it can apply to a great many people.

Mediums Say: Cold readers give vague and general information. We often get very specific pieces of information—initials, exact names, historical facts such as causes of death, personal descriptions such as size and appearance, personality characteristics such as shy or outgoing—that match the deceased loved ones of the sitters.

What the Experiments Actually Reveal: When the sitters carefully score the data for initials, names, historical facts, personal descriptions, personality characteristics, and the like, the data turn out to be very specific for individual sitters. This became clear when readings were scored by control groups; the control group accuracy ratings were consistently much lower.

Point 5: Lucky Guesses

Skeptics Speculate: The high rates of accuracy, if they occur, must reflect lucky guesses. These must be accidents, the result of fishing. They are not replicable.

Mediums Say: We are most definitely not guessing. We are getting specific sights, sounds, and feelings. Sometimes we interpret what we see, and sometimes the information is faint. But the process does not involve guessing.

What the Experiments Actually Reveal: Our experiments provided replication by having sitters read by as many as five mediums. After precise scoring, the findings showed remarkable replication across mediums and sitters, and across experiments, as well. Probability values extend from the millions to the trillions. Guessing and chance cannot account for the accuracy of the information being provided.

Point 6: Experimenter Biases or Mistakes

Skeptics Speculate: Either the experimenters are engaged in fraud or they must be deceiving themselves. They are somehow unconsciously influencing the results, giving information to the mediums or encouraging the sitters to inflate their ratings.

Mediums Say: The experimenters have all along been suspicious of us, never accepting on faith what we said but building ever-tighter controls to ensure the studies would be medium fraud-proof and sitter rater-proof. The scientists running the experiments are quite reluctant to believe, and they keep challenging our honesty and integrity.

What the Experiments Actually Reveal: Despite ever-tighter experimental controls, consistent efforts to have the raters give less favorable scores when in doubt, and, in [one particular] experiment, having the raters silently score their own transcripts as well as the other sitters' transcripts (thus eliminating any cues from the experimenters), the data still came out remarkably positive. Nonetheless, the experimenters are still uneasy about concluding that the data are genuine, reflecting their own cautious approach and their own fears.

Point 7: Motivation of the Mediums

Skeptics Say: Mediums are motivated to cheat the public; to take money from gullible, grieving people; and to be famous. They are participating in faulty lab experiments to feed their egos and raise their fees.

Mediums Say: The description of taking money from gullible people may fit some, perhaps many, who call themselves mediums. Those of us who have been involved in the experiments do this work because we have discovered a gift for it and because it helps people realize that life is eternal.

What the Experiments Actually Reveal: The mediums who participate in this research are putting their careers and reputations on the line. If we catch them cheating, we will expose them, in keeping with our lab motto of "If it is real, it will be revealed; if it is fake, we'll find the mistake." We have never found any evidence of fraud or cheating in our highly select group of research mediums. They know that if we ever do, they will be publicly embarrassed and their careers will suffer.

Point 8: Motivation of the Skeptics

Skeptics Say: Our motivation is to protect the public against fake mediums and voodoo science. Mediums are frauds, and scientists who study them are gullible or worse.

Mediums Say: The skeptics have their minds made up and are not willing to examine the data from the experiments. They are unwilling to be open-minded in the presence of compelling data.

What the Experiments Actually Reveal: Skeptics often ignore essential details of the scientific methods. They typically dismiss data that are positive, and they engage in irrational arguments to hold on to their personal beliefs. Extreme skeptics practice what could be termed voodoo skepticism, which lacks integrity and humility.

For example, the man who styles himself as the Amazing Randi, a "demystifier of paranormal and pseudoscientific claims," emphatically insists that all mediums "pretend" and engage in "deceptive art." He appears so committed to this view that even solid data will not change his mind. The professional skeptics have discovered that, as skeptics, they can make money selling books and magazines. Their careers are on the line.

Point 9: Mind-Reading by Mediums

Skeptics Speculate: If the mediums are doing anything paranormal, they must be reading the minds of the sitters. They can't be talking to dead people, because dead people are dead, period.

Mediums Say: If we were reading the minds of the sitters, we would get only the information the sitters know about and were hoping to receive. Often we get people the sitter knows but was not expecting. Sometimes we get information that the sitter thinks is wrong or doesn't know about, which later turns out to be correct.

What the Experiments Actually Reveal: Careful analysis of the experimental data shows many examples that mind-reading cannot explain—among them, who the sitters hope to hear from versus who they actually do hear from, information provided by the medium that is not anything the sitter had been thinking about, and information that the sitter did not know but was later able to confirm. Many such examples make it clear that telepathy cannot explain all the data.

Point 10: Memory in the Universe

Skeptics Speculate: Physics reminds us that light and energy extend into space, and photons as old as the birth of the universe have been recorded as "background" radiation. Maybe mediums, if they are doing something paranormal, are simply reading dead memory traces of information and energy in the universe

Mediums Say: Maybe we are reading some information from memory banks in the universe. However, it often doesn't feel like that. The information seems too alive and playful. Not only that, would dead memories disagree with us when we mishear or misinterpret what is communicated, as often happens in our readings?

What the Experiments Actually Reveal: The research to date does not eliminate a possible memory retrieval process from the "vacuum" of space. However, careful analysis of the language used by the mediums, plus examples like [one sitter's] deceased grandmother seemingly continuing to communicate during the reading for the subsequent sitter, suggests that the "information" is not static or "dead" like information stored on a hard drive or CD.

Point 11: Talking to Dead People

Skeptics Speculate: Since we know that death is final, what the mediums report must be their imagination. Or worse, the mediums are making it up. If the mediums really believe in what they are doing, they must be deceiving themselves.

Mediums Say: It truly feels as if we are talking to living souls. They seem as alive as the skeptics are, only usually more loving and accepting. Dead people often show us and tell us things that surprise us as well as the sitters. The deceased often correct us, contradicting the sitter.

What the Experiments Actually Reveal: In the experiments, information was consistently retrieved that can best be explained as coming from living souls. In [one] procedure, information was obtained before the medium ever spoke with the sitters. Information sometimes comes that the sitter disagrees with but that turns out to be correct. Also, mediums are sometimes corrected by deceased people. The data appear to be as valid, convincing and living as the mediums, sitters, skeptics, and scientists themselves.

That's what the experimental data unmistakably show.

Again, this analysis applies only to the mediums who have agreed to be the subjects of our controlled laboratory experiments: . . . Laurie Campbell, John Edward, Suzane Northrop, Anne Gehman, and George Anderson.

If there are five, there are probably many more.

Mediums Understand How Spirits Communicate

James Van Praagh

James Van Praagh has claimed to be a medium ever since child-hood. As an adult, his claim has expanded into books, CDs, talk shows, self-empowerment seminars, and a homepage at www. vanpraagh.com. He offers advice and guidance on healing and grief, and much of that advice comes through his contacts with spirits. Van Praagh claims that thousands of spirits are in con-tact with him. He also claims that the living need only give him a name, and he can then channel their deceased loved ones.

In this excerpt Van Praagh tells stories of how spirits have contacted him in a variety of ways. He aims to remove the black magic/occult stigma associated with spirits, instead positing them as earnest, peaceful entities.

Van Praagh presents these phenomena in a level-headed style with the gentle humor and mysticism that has made him popu-lar. He encourages everyone to get in touch with his or her psy-chic powers and even gives specific instructions. He believes that the average person needs to become more sensitive to his or her surroundings.

Van Praagh had a television show, Beyond with James Van Praagh, *which aired from 2002 to 2003 on the CBS television network. Similar to medium Allison DuBois, the inspiration for NBC's* Medium *series, Van Praagh is the coexecutive producer of the series* The Ghost Whisperer, *which premiered on CBS in 2005.*

After the success of my first book, *Talking to Heaven,* I was invited to appear on *The Oprah Winfrey Show.* Oprah ap-peared quite perplexed about the nature of communication

James Van Praagh, "Signals from Spirits: Various Methods Spirits Use to Contact Us," *Heaven and Earth.* New York: Simon & Schuster, 2001. Copyright © 2001 by Spiritual Horizons, Inc. All rights reserved. Reproduced by permission of Simon & Schuster Adult Publishing Group.

with the other side. She wanted to know why spirits could not clearly state their names and any pertinent information instead of my having to hear some random thoughts or see pictures.

My response to her was pretty much what I tell other people. First of all, we must realize that there are other levels of consciousness. This means that other dimensions and expressions of life exist beyond the physical one. The time-space ratio and other laws of physics may not apply to these other dimensions—they may be ruled by a system unknown to us. Therefore, spirits won't necessarily communicate in ways that we expect or are accustomed to.

Why Don't Spirits Communicate Clearly?

As I told Oprah, "Spirit communication is like speaking a foreign language. Images have unchanging meanings attached to them, whereas names do not." For instance, the names Jodie or White mean nothing because they are merely letters combined to make a sound. However, a car or a house has a meaning attached to it that is clear to anyone, no matter what language he or she speaks.

This doesn't mean that the interpretation of the images is always correct. Often, mediums misinterpret the pictures. For instance, a spirit tries to convey something to me about a necklace she is wearing. She fingers the locket attached to the gold chain around her neck. I may see her touching her throat but not see the locket. I interpret the picture as "something is the matter with her throat," which would be erroneous. Let's take another symbol, like clouds. I may see dark clouds and think "bad news," or white clouds and decide it means happiness. However, clouds may signify something else to the spirit, such as confusion. We must bear in mind that misinterpretation or misidentification of the images does not mean that we are not communicating with the spirit world. It means that we are not understanding the message correctly.

Furthermore, the spiritual landscape is *thought*. Therefore, spirits communicate to us through telepathic thoughts. As a mental medium, I "read" these thoughts as feelings, visions, and auditory impulses. I am able to interpret these messages through a common energy that permeates and transcends all levels of existence. I identify it as the God Force energy. Others call it prana. For lack of better words, this energy is love. Love is the ingredient that makes the communication on both ends strong and successful.

One must also realize that someone who has recently passed on is now in a completely unfamiliar world. A spirit may be a bit confused at first because the physical laws to which it had become accustomed no longer exist. Once a spirit recognizes that it is not *dead*, but very much alive— more alive than ever before—it learns that it lives in a world of thought. Thus a spirit must begin to understand how to use thought to create what it wants.

Once acclimated to their new world, spirits begin to hear our thoughts of grief, sadness, and regret. They see the pain and anguish brought on by their death. Knowing that they are still alive, albeit in another form, they want to reassure us that they are still aware of everything taking place on earth. This is not easy, because most of us are so overwhelmed with loss that the last thing we can think about is spirit communication.

Spirits and Mediums Have to Work Together

Depending upon a spirit's personality, abilities, and its own awareness, it will attempt in every way possible to communicate and get us to understand its newly relocated existence. I have often said at my workshops, "It's like they are playing spirit charades. Spirits are jumping up and down all around us frustratingly trying to communicate a message. And we just don't get it."

Another thing to understand is that a spirit can only draw upon a medium's own life experiences to communicate with that medium. In other words, my experiences become its reference tool. Since I can't tell the difference between a carburetor and a spark plug, it would be difficult for me to understand a spirit describe the inner workings of a car engine.

It is also necessary to remember that spirits communicate from a dimension that vibrates at a faster frequency than ours, and they tend to send their impressions more rapidly than what we are used to on earth. It's as if we are communicating across a vast chasm without the help of a simultaneous translator. It takes a lot of energy on both sides to converse with one another. That is why mediums must stay as focused as possible on the information a spirit is conveying. Often, mediums speak very quickly because they are trying to keep up with a spirit's rapid-fire messages. Over the years, I have learned to emphasize to spirits the need for accuracy in communication. I am constantly conveying to spirits that they must speak clearly and send the message as powerfully as they can.

People often ask, "Why do spirits say such trivial things? Why don't they tell us about the important meanings of life?" Spirits, like humans, have personalities, and use trivialities such as appearance, certain achievements, or even minor incidents to identify themselves. They convey trivial messages for their specificity, so that their loved ones will recognize them as "the real thing." Second, although spirits have an expanded consciousness on the other side, and are able to see every thought and action of their lifetime, their souls are still evolving. Until a soul reaches the higher heavens, its knowledge of life is still limited. Also, spirits will not interfere with our earthly lessons, either as individuals or as an entire planet of people. They will not hinder our spiritual growth by giving us the answers when it is our responsibility to make the correct choices for ourselves.

Spirits Make Contact in Many Ways

So how do spirits manifest their presence to us? Depending upon its ingenuity with manipulating energy and electromagnetic fields, there are many ways a spirit can pierce the dense energy of this slow-moving world called earth. It takes quite a lot of power to finesse these energetic patterns. As I said, spirits primarily use thought to get messages to us. Some of the more common mental means of communicating [are]: clairvoyance, clairaudience, and clairsentience. Other types of mental transmissions are dreams, inspirational thought, ..., and the Ouija board. ...

The Crossover: When You Dream About Someone Who Has Passed

People have asked me, "Why do spirits come in our dreams?" And, "Why can't they come when I am awake?" My answer is usually the same. Spirits come in our dreams for two reasons: To reassure us that they have survived physical death, and to let us know that they are a part of our lives and still love us. Perhaps they choose to enter our dream state because we are not in a rational mind-set and, therefore, are more accepting of their visit as a reality rather than as merely our wishful thinking. I often tell people who are unsure of their crossover visit to think about the dream. Did the spirit seem alive? Did the spirit appear as you remembered him or her? What was the spirit doing or saying? If the actions match the personality of a loved one, then it was probably that person.

Spirits Use Dreams to Send Messages

Besides using dreams to show that they still exist, spirits also use dreams to send us messages. Perhaps they are trying to help us get out of a bad situation or providing us with the answer to some problem that we are having at work.

The main characteristics of dreams are symbols, and it is important that we learn to understand these symbols. There are many books, and even more workshops and classes, about dream interpretation. However, we must understand that not all symbols mean the same thing to all people. A person living in New York City may feel more comforted by the sights and sounds of a busy city than by the stillness of a quiet country-side. For that reason, a country setting might represent loneli-ness to one person and tranquillity to another. Not everyone's symbolic vocabulary is the same; only you will know what a symbol means to you.

There are many types of dreams besides the typical sym-bolic dream. Clairvoyant dreams involve seeing visions that subsequently prove to be true. For instance, the other night I had a dream about an ornate building. The next day, as I drove to an appointment, I passed the same building that I had seen in my dream. I had never seen it before. When I talk about dreams in my workshops, someone inevitably comes to me at the end and shares a clairvoyant dream. One fellow said he dreamed of a friend he hadn't seen in ten years. "A few days later I saw my friend's name in the newspaper."

Prophetic dreams are usually about events that come to pass several days, weeks, or even years later. These dreams are rare for most people. However, there are some psychics who can predict earthquakes and other phenomena based on pro-phetic dreams.

Spirit guides, animal guides, and angels all use our dream state to send us messages. I have a friend whose dreams con-tain a variety of animals—mountain lions, bears, and alliga-tors.

"Why do I always dream about animals?" she once asked.

"They are temporary spirit guides," I replied. "Their mes-sage pertains to the particular experience you are going through at the time of the dream."

I told her to look up the animal in an encyclopedia—its message probably had to do with the characteristics of that particular species. For instance, a bear hibernates. My friend is prone to staying alone quite a bit, so maybe it was informing her that she was hibernating too much. . . .

Dream interpretation takes persistence and attention, but once you learn to remember quite a bit of your dreams, you will be on your way to intensifying your psychic awareness.

Inspirational Thought: When Spirits Give Us Thoughts

Inspiration means "in spirit." For a moment, think back to all the times you were driving a car, watching a television show, cooking, or bathing when, without warning, you thought about someone who had passed on. Or you came up with a solution to a certain situation. You later realized that if you hadn't followed through with your thoughts, you would have suffered some dire consequences. You might say that you were *inspired* to take action.

In this dimension, we rely on the limitations of the physical senses to communicate. But in our natural state of being, which is spirit, we communicate telepathically, by thought. When you pass into spirit, you no longer need vocal cords to transmit words, because your thoughts are immediately received by other individuals. Spirits make contact by imposing their thoughts into our consciousness. It's how they communicate. I like to call it spirit-to-spirit or mind-to-mind communication. . . .

Spirits are around us during much of our waking state, attempting to use thought to influence us to make the correct choices. Many times clients will say that before arriving for their appointments—either in the car on the way over or several days prior to our meeting—they somehow felt a spirit with them. Many people also become aware of spirit energy in times of distress. People will tell me, "I felt I was not alone." They declare that some unseen force or guardian angel was by their side.

We are inspired and encouraged by spirit every day and in every way. We need only be open to clearing our channels for transmission. . . .

A Ouija Board Can Call Good Spirits

I began using the Ouija board. . . . Instead of pen and paper, you use a board imprinted with the alphabet, numbers 0 to 9, and the words Yes and No. By placing your fingers lightly on a pointing device known as a planchette, you can begin receiving answers to your questions, spelled out letter by letter.

The Ouija board was one of the first instruments I used in my introduction to the world of spirit. There have been many fears and misconceptions that the Ouija board is a tool of evil. As always, when you delve into the world of the unknown, you must be cautious and properly prepare yourself to attract only the highest order of spirits. If you have a consciousness of fear and hate, you can be susceptible to the unwholesome energies and entities of the universe.

I always began the process of using the Ouija board within a consciousness of love. I would sit for several minutes and meditate to ground myself and raise my energy level. Then I would say a prayer for spiritual guidance, protection, and light. Before making any attempt to contact spirit with the Ouija board, always make sure to surround yourself with love. Then, if you feel a spirit has arrived to communicate, ask if the spirit is from the light. If it is not, it will usually depart.

One of my favorite experiences with the Ouija board happened when I was with my friend Drew. We had been friends for quite a while, and although he had seen me at several public demonstrations, he didn't know that I had also used the Ouija board to contact the other side.

We were at our friend Kelly's house, and her Ouija board was out in plain view, so I decided to show Drew how it was used. After I said a prayer, Kelly and I placed our fingers on the planchette, and immediately it started flying from one letter to another. We took turns asking questions, and Kelly received several messages from her mother.

Then Drew took her place. A woman who identified herself as Mary greeted us.

Drew said, "Mary is my deceased grandmother's name."

After giving Drew many messages of love, she closed by saying, "My son has a good heart."

Drew thought that her message about his father was very sweet. We all knew Drew's dad to be a very kind man.

The next week Drew called me from his parents' house. "I just took my father to the hospital. He has some kind of viral infection in his heart."

The next few days were touch and go, as Drew explained that he came close to losing his dad. However, it wasn't until Drew's last remark that the true meaning of the Ouija board's message became clear.

"The doctors feel he will pull through. They say it is because *he has a good heart.*"

Physical Phenomena

When physical phenomena are being used as a means, a message is projected through the use of material objects and the environment. This type of physical contact includes changes in room temperature, electrical occurrences, rapping and knocking, electronic voice phenomena, spirit lights, telephone and television communication, apparitions, materialization, spirit photography, trance mediumship, transfiguration and apports.

How does this occur? In physical phenomena, electromagnetic energy fields around us are rearranged either through our own conscious or unconscious efforts, or through a spirit's control. Under certain conditions, spirits are able to move the physical objects with which they come into contact. Usually this happens spontaneously. The power and force of these occurrences increase in an atmosphere where people are serious about spirit contact. The following are various methods of spirit communication using physical objects or the environment. . . .

Apparitions

Apparitions are phantom forms of people and animals, commonly known as ghosts. What is a ghost? A ghost is usually a recently departed spirit that has not yet adjusted to its new life on the other side. Thoughts of the deceased are projected outwardly and usually connect with loved ones, causing the living to, in essence, see the dead. Apparitions seem to move through solid material, to open doors or windows, and even to cause objects to fall off shelves. These souls are desperately trying to get the message of their existence across the dimensions. They often appear and disappear in an instant.

It is also common for the dying to see apparitions a few days before they pass on, as if being called to the other side by those already there.

However, some discarnate spirits can appear to total strangers as semisolid beings. Again one can only say that these souls are extremely attached to the physical plane, and they will linger in its atmosphere indefinitely.

Materialization

Materialization is the process by which solid material is created by the vital force of the members of a development group. A gauzelike, colorless and odorless substance known as ectoplasm will emerge from the ears, nose, mouth, or solar plexus area of the medium and form into "physical" matter. This can be a disembodied spirit or parts of a spirit. The spirit will possess all the properties and appearances of a physical body, and often will seem to have solid flesh and bones.

Ectoplasm is extremely sensitive and almost impossible to manifest in normal light. That is why physical mediums usually work in a dark environment. There are very few physical mediums on the earth today. . . .

Trances

Trance mediums are able to slow their brain waves to reach a deep level of relaxation. A trance state can be induced by meditation or hypnosis, and trance mediumship can be achieved only after extensive study. Depending on the medium, there are various degrees of a trance state, from light to very deep. When a medium is in this altered state, a guide or spirit will blend with his consciousness. Often the medium's voice pattern will change as the guide or spirit speaks through him. The same is true for a medium's handwriting when a spirit communicates through the written word. Channeling is similar to trance mediumship. . . .

Contacting a Spirit Is Possible

Signals from spirit may be elaborate or simple, but they are always around us. We need only to become sensitive to understand their meaning. When you are working with the invisible realms, remember that there is always a higher intelligence in charge. Not everything that you desire can be achieved because you want it to. We are here to live as best we can with integrity and responsibility. Within this framework it is possible to succeed in contacting the spirit world. Don't be discouraged. Certain things will be easier for you than others. Concentrate on developing those abilities that are natural and appropriate for you.

Fact or Fiction?

CHAPTER 2

The Evidence Against Mediums

The Skeptic's Dictionary Explains Claims Against Mediums

Robert T. Carroll

The Skeptic's Dictionary *started in 1994, when Robert T. Carroll was teaching a college course on critical thinking. He was also taking a course on Web design, so to put his new computer skills to the test, he started posting explanations of how to think critically about paranormal events. As of 2006, the dictionary has four hundred entries and has been published as a traditional book. Carroll estimates that the Web site receives more than a million visitors a month.*

In the following excerpt, Carroll gives a definition and overview of the term medium, *including comments on popular mediums seen on television. Explanations of* cold reading *and* hot reading *cover the usual skeptical take on these techniques.*

Carroll concludes that we believe in mediums because "human beings are very good at finding meaning where there is none and giving significance to what is actually meaningless in itself."

Robert T. Carroll is a professor at Sacramento City College. He is the author of Becoming a Critical Thinker.

Editor's Note: The following are entries from The Skeptic's Dictionary *and follow a dictionary format.*

Cold Reading

"In the course of a successful reading, the psychic may provide most of the words, but it is the client that provides most of the meaning and all of the significance."

—*Ian Rowland (2000: 60)*

Robert T. Carroll, "Cold Reading," "Hot Reading," "Medium," from *The Skeptic's Dictionary*, www.skepdic.com. Reproduced by permission.

Cold reading refers to a set of techniques used by professional manipulators to get a subject to behave in a certain way or to think that the cold reader has some sort of special ability that allows him to "mysteriously" know things about the subject. Cold reading goes beyond the usual tools of manipulation: suggestion and flattery. In cold reading, salespersons, hypnotists, advertising pros, faith healers, con men, and some therapists bank on their subject's inclination to find more meaning in a situation than there actually is. The desire to make sense out of experience can lead us to many wonderful discoveries, but it can also lead us to many follies. The manipulator knows that his mark will be inclined to try to make sense out of whatever he is told, no matter how farfetched or improbable. He knows, too, that people are generally self-centered, that we tend to have unrealistic views of ourselves, and that we will generally accept claims about us that reflect not how we are or even how we really think we are but how we wish we were or think we should be. He also knows that for every several claims he makes about you that you reject as being inaccurate, he will make one that meets with your approval; and he knows that you will remember the hits he makes and forget the misses.

Thus, a good manipulator can provide a reading of a total stranger, which will make the stranger feel that the manipulator possesses some special power. For example, Bertram Forer [a personality researcher] has never met you, the reader, yet he offers the following cold reading of you [taken from a newstand astrology book]:

> Some of your aspirations tend to be pretty unrealistic. At times you are extroverted, affable, sociable, while at other times you are introverted, wary and reserved. You have found it unwise to be too frank in revealing yourself to others. You pride yourself on being an independent thinker and do not accept others' opinions without satisfactory proof. You prefer a certain amount of change and variety, and become dis-

satisfied when hemmed in by restrictions and limitations. At times you have serious doubts as to whether you have made the right decision or done the right thing. Disciplined and controlled on the outside, you tend to be worrisome and insecure on the inside.

Your sexual adjustment has presented some problems for you. While you have some personality weaknesses, you are generally able to compensate for them. You have a great deal of unused capacity which you have not turned to your advantage. You have a tendency to be critical of yourself. You have a strong need for other people to like you and for them to admire you.

Here's another reading [from psychic Sydney Omarr]:

People close to you have been taking advantage of you. Your basic honesty has been getting in your way. Many opportunities that you have had offered to you in the past have had to be surrendered because you refuse to take advantage of others. You like to read books and articles to improve your mind. In fact, if you're not already in some sort of personal service business, you should be. You have an infinite capacity for understanding people's problems and you can sympathize with them. But you are firm when confronted with obstinacy or outright stupidity. Law enforcement would be another field you understand. Your sense of justice is quite strong.

The selectivity of the human mind is always at work. We pick and choose what data we will remember and what we will give significance to. In part, we do so because of what we already believe or want to believe. In part, we do so in order to make sense out of what we are experiencing. We are not manipulated simply because we are gullible or suggestible, or just because the signs and symbols of the manipulator are vague or ambiguous. Even when the signs are clear and we are skeptical, we can still be manipulated. In fact, it may even be the case that particularly bright persons are more likely to be manipulated when the language is clear and they are thinking logically. To make the connections that the manipulator wants you to make, you must be thinking logically. . . .

Cold-Reading Techniques

There seem to be three common factors in these kinds of readings. One factor involves fishing for details. The psychic says something at once vague and suggestive, e.g., "I'm getting a strong feeling about January here." If the subject responds, positively or negatively, the psychic's next move is to play off the response. E.g., if the subject says, "I was born in January" or "my mother died in January" then the psychic says something like "Yes, I can see that," anything to reinforce the idea that the psychic was more precise than he or she really was. If the subject responds negatively, e.g., "I can't think of anything particularly special about January," the psychic might reply, "Yes, I see that you've suppressed a memory about it. You don't want to be reminded of it. Something painful in January. Yes, I feel it. It's in the lower back [fishing] . . . oh, now it's in the heart [fishing] . . . umm, there seems to be a sharp pain in the head [fishing] . . . or the neck [fishing]." If the subject gives no response, the psychic can leave the area, having firmly implanted in everybody's mind that the psychic really did 'see' something but the subject's suppression of the event hinders both the psychic and the subject from realizing the specifics of it. If the subject gives a positive response to any of the fishing expeditions, the psychic follows up with more of "I see that very clearly, now. Yes, the feeling in the heart is getting stronger."

Fishing is a real art and a good mentalist carries a variety of bait in his memory. For example, professional mentalist and author of one of the best books on cold reading, Ian Rowland (2002), says that he has committed to memory such things as the most common male and female names and a list of items likely to be lying about the house, such as an old cal-

endar, a photo album, newspaper clippings, and so on. Rowland also works on certain themes that are likely to resonate
with most people who consult psychics: love, money, career,
health, and travel. Since cold reading can occur in many contexts, there are several tactics Rowland covers. But whether
one is working with astrology, graphology, palmistry, psy-
chometry, or Tarot cards, or whether one is channeling messages from the dead à la James Van Praagh, there are specific
techniques one can use to impress clients with one's ability to
know things that seem to require paranormal powers.

Another characteristic of these readings is that many
claims are put in vague statement form ("I'm getting a warm
feeling in the crotch area") or in the form of a question ("I
sense that you have strong feelings about someone in this
room. Am I right?") Most, but not all, of the specific claims
are provided by the subject himself.

Some experts on cold reading emphasize paying attention
to body language and such things as the dress of the client.

> The reader begins with generalities which are applicable to
> large segments of the population. He or she pays careful at-
> tention to reactions: words, body language, skin color,
> breathing patterns, dilation or contraction of the pupils of
> the eye, and more. The subject of the reading will usually
> convey important information to the reader: sometimes in
> words, and sometimes in bodily reactions to the reading.

> From observation, the reader will feed back to the subject
> what the latter wants to hear. That is the overwhelming
> guiding principle of the mystics: Tell 'em what they want to
> hear. That will keep them coming back for more (Steiner
> 1989: 21).

Also, those occasions where the psychic has guessed
wrongly about the subject are likely to be forgotten by the
subject and the audience. What will be remembered are the
seeming hits, giving the overall impression of "wow, how else

could she have known all this stuff unless she is psychic." This same phenomenon of suppression of contrary evidence and selective thinking is so predominant in every form of psychic demonstration that it seems to be related to the old psychological principle: a man sees what he wants to see and disregards the rest.

Clients Make Cold Reading Successful

Many cold readings do not involve fishing, vagueness, or wild guessing. The key to a successful cold reading is the willingness, ability, and effort of the client to find meaning and significance in the words of the psychic, astrologer, palm reader, medium, or the like. A medium claiming to get messages from the dead might throw out a string of ambiguous images to the client. Father figure, the month of May, the Big-H, and H with an N sound, Henna, Henry, M, maybe Michael, teaching, books, maybe something published. This list could mean different things to different people. To some people it probably has no meaning. The client will either connect these dots or she won't. Clients of mediums who claim to get messages from the dead are very highly motivated clients. Not only do they have an implicit desire for immortality, they have an explicit desire to contact a dear loved one who has died. The odds are in favor of the medium that the client will find meaning in many different sets of ambiguous words and phrases. If she connects just a couple of them, she may be satisfied that the medium has made a connection to a dead relative. If she doesn't find any meaning or significance in the string, the medium still wins. He can try another string. He can insist that there's meaning here but the client just isn't trying hard enough to figure it out. He can suggest that some uninvited spirit guests are confusing the issue. It's a win-win situation for the medium because the burden is not on him but on the client to find the meaning and significance of the words.

Successful cold readings are sometimes a testament to the skills of the reader, but they are always a testament to the ability of human beings to make sense out of the most disparate of data. The skill of cold reading can be honed and turned into an art, as it is by professionals who work as mediums, palm readers, astrologers, and the like. Many of these professionals may not even realize what they are doing and attribute their high rate of client satisfaction to the truth of astrology or palmistry. They may come to believe in the reality of the spirit world by becoming convinced that meaningful signals from beyond sometimes rise above the noise of daily life and are detected by skilled mediums. Some of these professionals know what they are doing and they deceive the public, if not themselves. Other professionals know what they are doing but they tell their clients or audiences after their performances that they need no paranormal or supernatural powers to accomplish their feats.

Cold Reading Deceives All Involved

In evaluating cold reading, it is a common mistake to focus mainly on the reader. Gary Schwartz seems to have done this in his book *The Afterlife Experiments: Breakthrough Scientific Evidence of Life After Death*. He seems to think that if he can eliminate trickery, deceit (cold reading), and fraud (hot reading) on the part of the mediums in his experiments, then he has eliminated cold reading as a viable explanation for the validation of readings by sitters (those who sit for a reading). He makes this point throughout his book and emphasizes it in a paper he and others published in the *Journal of the Society for Psychical Research*:

> Because the sitter-silent condition provides no verbal/semantic feedback to the mediums as well as minimal nonverbal feedback (save for possible sighs or breathing information from the sitters), the sitter-silent condition eliminates the plausibility of 'cold reading' as a probable explanation

for the findings. For this reason, the paper reports the data from the sitter-silent condition. These form the most compelling evidence for anomalous information retrieval.

The sitter-silent condition (a.k.a. the Russek Protocol) lets the medium do a reading within hearing distance of the sitter but does not permit the medium to ask any questions or the sitter to make any responses during the reading.

It is evident from tests done on college students who are given personality or astrological readings, that it is not necessary to interrogate the client to get him or her to find meaning and significance in complete sentences that were not generated on the basis of any personal knowledge. It also seems evident that many people should be able to find meaning and significance in various strings of initials, names, descriptions of places, and so on. And, while it is true that some mediums use trickery, such as having accomplices in the audience or having detective work done on the sitter, it is not necessary. What many saw [medium] Rosemary Althea do in a Penn & Teller *Bullshit!* episode [the television series that features the magicians and attempts to debunk supernatural and other claims], for example, is not required for a successful reading. Her agent brought a couple whose child had committed suicide to a reading (guess what came through in the reading) and she chatted up a young man before the reading began who told her that he wanted to connect with his mother (guess who she connected to during the reading). In the same *Bullshit!* episode, Mark Edward (no relation to John Edward) did a successful reading for a woman without using any hot reading tricks. But even his method of fishing around for something the sitter can connect to isn't necessary for a successful reading. The sitter is the key to the success of a reading by a medium and different mediums use different methods.

Successful readings that involve contact with dead loved ones are a testament to the wonderful capacity of our species to find meaning in just about any image, word, phrase, or string of such items. We can find Jesus in a burnt tortilla, Mother Teresa in a cinnamon bun, the Virgin Mary in a water stain or in the discoloration on the bark of a tree, or Vladimir Lenin in the soap scum on a shower curtain (pareidolia). We can see the devil in a puddle of water and hear him tempting us (apophenia). It is the same complex human brain that makes it possible for us to find these illusory meanings that allows us to write and appreciate multifaceted poetry and to discover real patterns in nature. This wonderful brain of ours, the product of tens of thousands of years of evolution, also makes it possible for us to deceive ourselves and others. Even more wonderful is the fact that this brain of ours can be used to try to understand the many ways we go right and wrong in our attempts to make sense out of life and death. . . .

Hot Reading

Hot reading is a technique used by psychics, mediums, palm readers, and the like that involves surreptitiously gaining information from clients. For example, a medium who claims to get messages from the dead will chat up the audience members before a performance and gather information from them. Later, when the psychic does a reading and seems to make contact with a young man's mother, even the young man won't remember that he told the psychic before the show that he wanted to connect with his mother. The psychic might have her agent bring a couple to the performance and when the psychic reveals to all that the couple's son committed suicide, everyone is convinced she's made contact. She may have [but it was] with her agent before the show to get this information. (See Penn & Teller's *Bullshit!*, episode one of the first season.)

At least one faith healer, Peter Popoff, has pretended to get messages from God when he was really getting messages from his wife via an earpiece (Randi 1989: ch. 9; "Secrets of the Psychics").

Some palm readers might go through a client's purse or have an accomplice do so, in order to garner information about the client. For a detailed description of the lengths to which some psychics will go to get information about clients see M. Lamar Keene's *The Psychic Mafia* (1997).

Medium

"...We [psychics] are here to heal people and to help people grow; ... skeptics ... they're just here to destroy people. They're not here to encourage people, to enlighten people. They're here to destroy people."

—*James Van Praagh on "Larry King Live," March 6, 2001*

"Death is a part of life, and pretending that the dead are gathering in a television studio in New York to talk twaddle with a former ballroom-dance instructor is an insult to the intelligence and humanity of the living."

—*Michael Shermer*

In spiritualism, a medium is one with whom spirits communicate directly. In an earlier, simpler but more dramatic age, a good medium would produce voices or apports, ring bells, float or move things across a darkened room, produce automatic writing or ectoplasm, and, in short, provide good entertainment value for the money.

Today, a medium is likely to write bathetic inspirational books and say he or she is channeling, such as J.Z. Knight and the White Book of her Ramtha from Atlantis. Today's most successful mediums, however, simply claim the dead communicate through them. Under a thin guise of doing "spiritual healing" and "grief counseling," they use traditional cold reading techniques and sometimes surreptitiously gathered information about their subjects to give the appearance of transmitting comforting messages from the dead. Subjective validation plays a key role in this kind of mediumship: The mediums rely upon the strong motivation of their clients to validate words, initials, statements or signs as accurate. The clients' success at finding significance and meaning in the sounds made by the medium are taken as evidence of contact with the dead.

Using the information provided them by their clients either during the cold reading or from other sources, such as conversations with the subjects before the readings or during breaks from studio sessions, they are able to convince many clients that they are getting messages from their dead loved ones. The medium passes on messages from the dead such as "he forgives you" or reveals things that are already known but leave the client wondering how did he know that? In the good old days of séances and elaborate trickery, a spiritualist fraud would be more likely to pass on the message "give more money to me and my group" (Keene 1997).

The Potential for Profit

Today, it is unnecessary to be so crude as to directly ask for money or prey upon elderly persons who have lots of cash and little time. People are literally waiting for years to give money to those who give hope that a dead loved one will communicate with them. There is also a lucrative book business for those who have messages from the dead and there is good money to be made by doing live shows for hundreds or thousands of people, each of whom pays $25 to $50 for the chance to connect with a lost child, spouse, or parent. There are also television opportunities for some mediums.

George Anderson, a former switchboard operator and author of *Lessons from the Light: Extraordinary Messages of Comfort and Hope from the Other Side* (2000), got his own ABC special featuring celebrities who wanted to contact the dead. Some mediums even get their own syndicated television programs, such as John Edward and James Van Praagh, although the latter's show was canned by Tribune Media Services after only a few episodes.

John Edward established himself as the first clairaudient to have his own show that featured deceased loved ones contacting audience members: "Crossing Over with John Edward" on the Sci-Fi Channel. Edward has been described as a fraud by James Randi [*Skeptic*, v. 8, no. 3] and Leon Jaroff [*Time*, March 5, 2001], to no avail. He may be a fraud, but he is an attractive and impressive one. Edward's show was syndicated and for some time he joined Xena the Warrior Princess and Jerry Springer on the USA Network. [Edward's show was canceled in 2004.]

James Van Praagh is a self-proclaimed medium who claims he has a gift that allows him to hear messages from just about anyone who is dead. According to Van Praagh, all the billions and billions and billions of dead people are just waiting for someone to give him their names. That's all it takes. Give Van Praagh a name, any name, and he will claim that some dead person going by that name is contacting him in words, fragments of sentences, or that he can feel their presence in a specific location. He has appeared on "Larry King Live," where he claimed he could feel the presence of Larry's dead parents. He even indicated where in the room this "presence" was coming from. He took phone calls on the air and, once given a name, started telling the audience what he was "hearing" or "feeling." Van Praagh plays a kind of twenty-questions game with his audience. He goes fishing, rapidly casting his baited questions one after the other until he gets a bite. Then he reels the fish in. Sometimes he falters, but most of the fish don't get away. He just rebaits and goes after the fish again until he rehooks. The fish love it. They reward Van Praagh's hard work by giving him positive feedback. This makes it appear to some that he is being contacted by spirits who are telling him that being dead is good, that they love those they left behind, and that they are sorry and forgive them everything.

What the Skeptics Say

Michael Shermer of *Skeptic* magazine calls Van Praagh "the master of cold-reading in the psychic world." Sociologist and student of anomalies, Marcello Truzzi of Eastern Michigan University, was less charitable. Truzzi studied characters like Van Praagh for more than 35 years and describes Van Praagh's demonstrations as "extremely unimpressive." ("A Spirited Debate," Dru Sefton, Knight Ridder News Service, *The San Diego Union-Tribune*, July 10, 1998, p. E1.) Truzzi said that most of what Van Praagh gives out is "twaddle," but it is good twaddle since "what people want is comfort, guilt assuagement. And they get that: Your parents love you; they forgive you; they look forward to seeing you; it's not your fault they're dead."

In *Why People Believe Weird Things* Shermer describes Van Praagh's success and how he wowed audiences on NBC's New Age talk show *The Other Side*. Shermer also tells us how he debunked Van Praagh on *Unsolved Mysteries*. Yet, no one in the audience was sympathetic to Shermer. One woman even told him that his behavior was "inappropriate" because he was destroying people's hopes in their time of grief.

Van Praagh has books out with can't-miss titles: *Talking to Heaven* and *Reaching to Heaven*, as well as *Healing Grief*. (*Talking to God* and *Talking to Angels* have already been taken.) His website keeps us informed of his books, tapes (e.g., *Develop Your Psychic-Self*), upcoming products (e.g., a series of meditation tapes), tours and appearances. Van Praagh and mediums like him can expect that their success will continue as long as they never tell a client that his parents forgive him for torturing them while they were alive or that it's time to admit to the murder. There is little chance of that happening, however.

In an interview with Dru Sefton, Van Praagh states that "there is no death, there is only life. . . . Every person is psychic or intuitive to a degree," and most spirits end up in heaven (Sefton 1998). These claims seem to based on nothing more than the belief that this is what many people want to hear.

Another devotee of Van Praagh is Charles Grodin, whose talk show on CNBC was cancelled shortly after Van Praagh's second appearance. Grodin demonstrated how open-minded, gullible, and devoted to his dead mother he is, as he fawned over the man who talks to heaven. Van Praagh's performance on Grodin's show was less than heavenly, but it was enough to satisfy Grodin and at least one couple in the audience who seemed to believe that their dead daughter was talking to Van Praagh. The only skepticism shown by Grodin was in wondering whether Van Praagh wasn't really reading the minds of the audience and the callers, rather than getting his messages from "the other side". The only person on the show who stated her doubts about the authenticity of Van Praagh's contact was a woman who lost a daughter to murder by terrorist Timothy McVeigh in the Oklahoma City bombing. She stated that nothing Van Praagh said rang true about her daughter except some generalities. The woman also claimed that her daughter communicates to her directly.

Mediums Are Unimpressive

When Van Praagh, Edward, Sylvia Browne or some other medium can't get a good bite, they remind the audience that sometimes the message is in fragments, sometimes they don't understand it, sometimes they misinterpret it, etc. If they're wrong, don't blame them since they never claimed to be perfect. Van Praagh seemed particularly inept on the Grodin show. He was not very artful. He used his usual bait: questions about girls and grandmothers, changes in the home, unresolved feelings, etc. He claimed to get messages about the usual stuff: angels, cancer, the heart, newspapers. What saves him much of the time is shotgunning, which ends with the ambiguous question "am I right?" and the client saying "yes," though we have no idea what the "yes" is in response to.

Van Praagh's shows are unimpressive to a skeptic, but to someone like Charles Grodin, who obviously is still deeply grieving his mother's death, he is a saint. Grodin practically asked for Van Praagh's blessing as he thanked him for his wonderful work. Hopefully, some in the audience were left wondering why there wasn't more skepticism shown.

Currently, there is a three-year wait for a private session with Van Praagh. However, there may be some dissatisfaction in Heaven, as several others on Earth have got the message [and] are now getting messages from the dead, too.

One of the more successful mediums is Allison Dubois, whose success multiplied when NBC showcased "Medium," a program said to be based on Dubois's psychic exploits. On her website, Dubois says:

"I call things like I see them and I am not afraid to push the boundaries of my abilities under university research conditions. I pride myself on accuracy, consistency and easing the pain of those who have lost loved ones."

In other words, she is cut from the same cloth as John Edward, George Anderson, Laurie Campbell, James Van Praagh, and a host of other "grief counselors" who offer their services to the grieving and the bewildered, for a fee of course. And like Edward, Anderson, and Campbell, Dubois has been tested by Gary Schwartz and declared by him to be a bona fide psychic.

Mediums Distort Accuracy

One reason we should distrust Schwartz's evaluation of anyone's psychic ability is his persistent revelation that he has little or no understanding of how subjective validation works. In a classic experiment that has been repeated many times in many different contexts, Bertram Forer gave a personality test to his students, ignored their answers, and gave each student an "evaluation" he had taken from a newsstand astrology column. He asked his students to evaluate the evaluation from 0 to 5, with "5" meaning the recipient felt the evaluation was an "excellent" assessment and "4" meaning the assessment was "good." The class average evaluation was 4.26. That was in 1948. The test has been repeated hundreds of time with psychology students and the average is still around 4.2. We might translate this to mean that it is quite common for people to be given strings of statements that are not based on any knowledge of the person and yet they commonly rate the statements as something like 80% accurate. Similar experiments have been done with phony biorhythm charts, graphology readings, astrological charts, and who knows what else.

According to Schwartz, when he tested Dubois she "always scored in the near-80 percent range. That clearly puts her among the best of the best" (McClain 2005).

However, without a control, Schwartz has no way of knowing whether Dubois's scores are extraordinarily high or just average. But even without the validation of someone of Schwartz's caliber, the motivation to make contact with departed loved ones is stronger by far than the drive to scrutinize the work of a scientist with a Ph.D. from Harvard University whose motto is Veritas [truth].

References

1. M. Lamar Keene, *The Psychic Mafia*. Amberst, NY: Prometheus, 1997.
2. Carla McClain, "Varied Readings on Arizona Psychic," *Arizona Daily Star*, January 17, 2005.
3. James Randi, *Flim-Flam!* Buffalo, NY: Prometheus, 1982.
4. James Randi, *The Faith Healers*. Buffalo, NY: Prometheus, 1982.
5. Ian Rowland, *The Full Facts Book of Cold Reading*. 3rd. ed. 2000.
6. Dru Sefton, "A Spirited Debate," *San Diego Union-Tribune*, July 10, 1998.
7. Michael Shermer, *Why People Believe Weird Things: Pseudoscience, Supersitution, and Other Confusions of Our Time*. New York: W.H. Freeman, 1997.
8. Robert A. Steiner, *Don't Get Taken!—Bunco and Bunkum Exposed—How to Protect Yourself*. Wide-Awake, 1989.

Mediums Are Frauds

Joe Nickell

This excerpt is from the popular magazine Skeptical Inquirer. *Staff journalists investigate current paranormal topics and come to skeptical, science-based conclusions. The reports are backed by extensive research dependent on science, rationality, and logic.*

At the time that this article was written, at the end of 2001, mediums were in their heyday on television. The most notable was John Edward, host of the immensely popular Crossing Over *series. Investigator Joe Nickell comments on the Edward phenomenon, but he also traces the history of deception, dishonesty, and outright fraud in the time line of mediums' rise to fame. He offers this history in order to show newcomers that the current crop of television mediums are just using the same old tricks.*

Nickell analyzes transcripts from an episode of Larry King Live *to show how mediums use a technique called cold reading, which is "an artful method of gleaning information from the sitter, then feeding it back as mystical revelation." He also cites a* Time *magazine article that suggests that mediums use "hot reading," which means they gather information directly from the audience prior to taping. Finally, he references an episode of* Dateline *in which a reporter gets John Edward to admit that he received information from a participant before taping began—information that Edward later played off as coming from a spirit. Nickell concludes that despite such evidence, people attending televised readings feel pressure to believe because they want to make their experience worthwhile. Mediums, he says, use this psychological pressure to their advantage.*

Nickell, who has written extensively on the paranormal, is a frequent contributor to Skeptical Inquirer.

Superstar "psychic medium" John Edward is a stand-up guy. Unlike the spiritualists of yore, who typically plied their trade in dark-room séances, Edward and his ilk often perform before live audiences and even under the glare of TV lights. Indeed, Edward (a pseudonym: he was born John MaGee Jr.) has his own popular show on the SciFi channel called *Crossing Over*, which has gone into national syndication (Barrett 2001; Mui 2001). I was asked by television newsmagazine *Dateline NBC* to study Edward's act: was he really talking to the dead?

The Spiritualism Craze

Today's spiritualism traces its roots to 1848 and the schoolgirl antics of the Fox sisters, Maggie and Katie. They seemed to communicate with the ghost of a murdered peddler by means of mysterious rapping sounds. Four decades later the foxy sisters confessed how they had produced the noises by trickery (Nickell 1994), but meanwhile others discovered they too could be "mediums" (those who supposedly communicate with the dead).

The "spiritualism" craze spread across the United States, Europe, and beyond. In darkened séance rooms, lecture halls, and theaters, various "spirit" phenomena occurred. The Davenport Brothers conjured up spirit entities to play musical instruments while the two mediums were, apparently, securely tied in a special "spirit cabinet." Unfortunately the Davenports were exposed many times, once by a local printer. He visited their spook show and volunteered as part of an audience committee to help secure the two mediums. He took that opportunity to secretly place some printer's ink on the neck of a violin, and after the séance one of the duo had his shoulder smeared with the black substance (Nickell 1999).

In Boston, while photographer William H. Mumler was recycling some glass photographic plates, he accidentally obtained faint images of previous sitters. He soon adapted the technique to producing "spirit extras" in photographs of his clients. But Mumler's scam was revealed when some of his ethereal entities were recognized as living Boston residents (Nickell 1994).

The great magician Harry Houdini (1874–1926) crusaded against phony spiritualists, seeking out elderly mediums who taught him the tricks of the trade. For example, while sitters touched hands around the séance table, mediums had clever ways of gaining the use of one hand. (One method was to slowly move the hands close together so that the fingers of one could be substituted for those of the other.) This allowed the production of special effects, such as causing a tin trumpet to appear to be levitating. Houdini gave public demonstrations of the deceptions. "Do Spirits Return?" asked one of his posters. "Houdini Says No—and Proves It" (Gibson 1977, 157).

Continuing the tradition, I have investigated various mediums, sometimes attending séances undercover and once obtaining police warrants against a fraudulent medium from the notorious Camp Chesterfield spiritualist center in Indiana (Nickell 1998). The camp is the subject of the book *The Psychic Mafia*, written by a former medium who recanted and revealed the tricks of floating trumpets (with disembodied voices), ghostly apparitions, materializing "apports," and other fake phenomena (Keene 1976)—some of which I have also witnessed firsthand.

The New Breed of Mediums

The new breed of spiritualists—like Edward, James Van Praagh, Rosemary Altea, Sylvia Browne, and George Anderson—avoid the physical approach with its risks of exposure and possible criminal charges. Instead they opt for the comparatively safe "mental mediumship" which involves the purported use of psychic ability to obtain messages from the spirit realm.

This is not a new approach, since mediums have long done readings for their credulous clients. In the early days they exhibited "the classic form of trance mediumship, as practiced by shamans and oracles," giving spoken "'spirit messages' that ranged all the way from personal (and sometimes strikingly accurate) trivia to hours-long public trance-lectures on subjects of the deepest philosophical and religious import" (McHargue 1972).

Some mediums produced "automatic" or "trance" or "spirit" writing, which the entities supposedly dictated to the medium or produced by guiding his or her hand. Such writings could be in flowery language indeed, as in this excerpt from one spirit writing in my collection:

> Oh my Brother—I am so glad to be able to come here with you and hold sweet communion for it has been a long time since I have controlled this medium but I remember how well used I had become to her magnetism[,] but we will soon get accustomed to her again and then renew the pleasant times we used to have. I want to assure you that we are all here with you this afternoon[—]Father[,] Mother[,] little Alice[—]and so glad to find it so well with you and we hope and feel dear Brother that you have seen the darkest part of life and that times are not with you now as they have been. . . .

and so on in this talkative fashion.

By contrast, today's spirits—whom John Edward and his fellow mediums supposedly contact—seem to have poor memories and difficulty communicating. For example, in one of his on-air séances (on *Larry King Live*, June 19, 1998), Edward said: "I feel like there's a J- or G-sounding name attached to this." He also perceived "Linda or Lindy or Leslie; who's this L name?" Again, he got a "Maggie or Margie, or some M-G-sounding name," and yet again heard from "either Ellen or Helen, or Eleanore—it's like an Ellen-sounding name."

Gone is the clear-speaking eloquence of yore; the dead now seem to mumble.

The spirits also seemingly communicate to Edward et al. as if they were engaging in pantomime. As Edward said of one alleged spirit communicant, in a *Dateline* session: "He's pointing to his head; something had to affect the mind or the head, from what he's showing me." No longer, apparently, can the dead speak in flowing Victorian sentences, but instead are reduced to gestures, as if playing a game of charades.

Cold Readings: An Old Trick

One suspects, of course, that it is not the imagined spirits who have changed but rather the approach today's mediums have chosen to employ. It is, indeed, a shrewd technique known as "cold reading"—so named because the subject walks in "cold"; that is, the medium lacks advance information about the person (Gresham 1953). It is an artful method of gleaning information from the sitter, then feeding it back as mystical revelation.

The "psychic" can obtain clues by observing dress and body language (noting expressions that indicate when one is on or off track), asking questions (which if correct will appear as "hits" but otherwise will seem innocent queries), and inviting the subject to interpret the vague statements offered. For example, nearly anyone can respond to the mention of a common object (like a ring or watch) with a personal recollection that can seem to transform the mention into a hit. (For more on cold reading see Gresham 1953; Hyman 1977; Nickell 2000.)...

Hot Reading, or "Mediumistic Espionage"

Although cold reading is the main technique of the new spiritualists, they can also employ "hot" reading on occasion. Houdini (1924) exposed many of these information-gathering techniques including using planted microphones to listen in on clients as they gathered in the mediums' anterooms—a technique Houdini himself used to impress visitors with his "telepathy" (Gibson 1976, 13). Reformed medium M. Lamar Keene's *The Psychic Mafia* (1976) describes such methods as conducting advance research on clients, sharing other mediums' files (what Keene terms "mediumistic espionage"), noting casual remarks made in conversation before a reading, and so on.

An article in *Time* magazine suggested John Edward may have used just such chicanery. One subject, a marketing manager named Michael O'Neill had received apparent messages from his dead grandfather but, when his segment aired, he noted that it had been improved through editing. According to *Time*'s Leon Jaroff (2001):

> Now suspicious, O'Neill recalled that while the audience was waiting to be seated, Edward's aides were scurrying about, striking up conversations and getting people to fill out cards with their name, family tree and other facts. Once inside the auditorium, where each family was directed to preassigned seats, more than an hour passed before show time while "technical difficulties" backstage were corrected.

Edward has a policy of not responding to criticism, but the executive producer of *Crossing Over* insists: "No information is given to John Edward about the members of the audience with whom he talks. There is no eavesdropping on gallery conversations, and there are no 'tricks' to feed information to John." He labeled the *Time* article "a mix of erroneous observations and baseless theories" (Nordlander 2001).

Caught in the Act?

Be that as it may, on *Dateline* Edward was actually caught in an attempt to pass off previously gained knowledge as spirit revelation. During the session he said of the spirits, "They're telling me to acknowledge Anthony," and when the cameraman signaled that was his name, Edward seemed surprised, asking "That's you? Really?" He further queried: "Had you not seen Dad before he passed? Had you either been away or been distanced?" Later, playing the taped segment for me, *Dateline* reporter John Hockenberry challenged me with Edward's apparent hit: "He got Anthony. That's pretty good." I agreed but added, "We've seen mediums who mill about before sessions and greet people and chat with them and pick up things."

Indeed, it turned out that that is just what Edward had done. Hours before the group reading, Tony had been the cameraman on another Edward shoot (recording him at his hobby, ballroom dancing). Significantly, the two men had chatted and Edward had obtained useful bits of information that he afterward pretended had come from the spirits. In a follow-up interview Hockenberry revealed the fact and grilled an evasive Edward:

Hockenberry: So were you aware that his dad had died before you did his reading?

Mr. Edward: I think he—I think earlier in the—in the day, he had said something.

Hockenberry: It makes me feel like, you know, that that's fairly significant. I mean, you knew that he had a dead relative and you knew it was the dad.

Mr. Edward: OK.

Hockenberry: So that's not some energy coming through, that's something you knew going in. You knew his name was Tony and you knew that his dad had died and you knew that he was in the room, right? That gets you . . .

Mr. Edward: That's a whole lot of thinking you got me doing, then. Like I said, I react to what's coming through, what I see, hear and feel. I interpret what I'm seeing, hearing and feeling, and I define it. He raised his hand, it made sense for him. Great.

Hockenberry: But a cynic would look at that and go, 'Hey,' you know, 'He knows it's the cameraman, he knows it's DATELINE. You know, wouldn't that be impressive if he can get the cameraman to cry?'

Mr. Edward: Absolutely not. Absolutely not. Not at all.

. . . In his . . . book *Crossing Over*, Edward tries to minimize the *Dateline* exposé, and in so doing breaks his own rule of not responding to criticism. He rebukes Hockenberry for "his big Gotcha! moment," adding:

Hockenberry came down on the side of the professional skeptic they used as my foil. He was identified as Joe Nickell, a member of the Committee for the Scientific Investigation of Claims of the Paranormal, which likes to simplify things and call itself CSICOP. He did the usual sound bites: that modern mediums are fast-talkers on fishing expeditions making money on people's grief—"the same old dogs with new tricks," in Hockenberry's words.

Edward claims to ignore any advance information that he may get from those he reads, but concedes, "it's futile to say this to a tough skeptic" (Edward 2001, 242–243).

Edward may have benefitted from actual information on another occasion, while undergoing a "scientific" test of his alleged powers (Schwartz et al. 2001). In video clips shown on *Dateline*, Edward was reading subjects—who were brought into the hotel room where he sat with his back to the door—when he impressed his tester with an atypical revelation. Edward stated he was "being shown the movie *Pretty in Pink* " and asked if there was "a pink connection." Then he queried, "Are you, like, wearing all pink?" The unidentified man acknowledged that he was. Yet Edward had thought the subject was a woman, and I suspect that erroneous guess was because of the color of his attire; I further suspect Edward *knew* it was pink, that as the man entered the room Edward glimpsed a flash of the color as it was reflected off some shiny surface, such as the glass of a picture frame, the lens of the video camera, etc. I challenge Edward to demonstrate his reputed color-divining ability under suitably controlled conditions that I will set up.

The Pressure to Believe

In addition to shrewd cold reading and out-and-out cheating, "psychics" and "mediums" can also boost their apparent accuracy in other ways. They get something of a free ride from the tendency of credulous folk to count the apparent hits and ignore the misses. In the case of Edward, my analysis of 125 statements or pseudostatements (i.e., questions) he made on a *Larry King Live* program (June 19, 1998) showed that he was incorrect about as often as he was right and that his hits were mostly weak ones. (For example he mentioned "an older female" with "an M-sounding name," either an aunt or grandmother, he stated, and the caller supplied "Mavis" without identifying the relationship; see Nickell 1998.)

Another session—for an episode of *Crossing Over* attended by a reporter for *The New York Times Magazine*, Chris Ballard (2001)—had Edward "hitting well below 50 percent for the day." Indeed, he twice spent "upward of 20 minutes stuck on one person, shooting blanks but not accepting the negative responses." This is a common technique: persisting in an attempt to redeem error, cajoling or even browbeating a sitter (as Sylvia Browne often does), or at least making the incorrect responses seem the person's fault. "Do not *not* honor him!" Edward exclaimed at one point, then (according to Ballard) "staring down the bewildered man."

When the taped episode actually aired, the two lengthy failed readings had been edited out, along with second-rate offerings. What remained were two of the best readings of the show (Ballard 2001). This seems to confirm the allegation in the *Time* article that episodes were edited to make Edward seem more accurate, even reportedly splicing in clips of one sitter nodding yes "after statements with which he remembers disagreeing" (Jaroff 2001).

Edited or not, sessions involving a group offer increased chances for success. By tossing out a statement and indicating a section of the audience rather than an individual, the performing "medium" makes it many times more likely that someone will "acknowledge" it as a "hit." Sometimes multiple audience members will acknowledge an offering, whereupon the performer typically narrows the choice down to a single person and builds on the success. Edward uses just such a technique (Ballard 2001).

Still another ploy used by Edward and his fellow "psychic mediums" is to suggest that people who cannot acknowledge a hit may find a connection later. "Write this down," an insistent Edward sometimes says, or in some other way suggests the person study the apparent miss. He may become even more insistent, the positive reinforcement diverting attention from the failure and giving the person an opportunity to find some adaptable meaning later (Nickell 1998).

Who Has the Burden of Proof?

Some skeptics believe the way to counter Edward and his ilk is to reproduce his effect, to demonstrate the cold-reading technique to radio and TV audiences. Of course that approach is unconvincing unless one actually poses as a medium and then—after seemingly making contact with subjects' dead loved ones—reveals the deception. Although audiences typically fall for the trick (witness *Inside Edition*'s use of it), I deliberately avoid this approach for a variety of reasons, largely because of ethical concerns. I rather agree with Houdini (1924, xi) who had done spiritualistic stunts during his early career:

> At the time I appreciated the fact that I surprised my clients, but while aware of the fact that I was *deceiving* them I did not see or understand the seriousness of trifling with such sacred sentimentality and the baneful result which inevitably

followed. To me it was a lark. I was a mystifier and as such my ambition was being gratified and my love for a mild sensation satisfied. After delving deep I realized the seriousness of it all. As I advanced to riper years of experience I was brought to a realization of the seriousness of trifling with the hallowed reverence which the average human being bestows on the departed, and when I personally became afflicted with similar grief I was chagrined that I should ever have been guilty of such frivolity and for the first time realized that it bordered on crime.

Of course tricking people in order to educate them is not the same as deceiving them for crass personal gain, but to toy with their deepest emotions—however briefly and well intentioned—is to cross a line I prefer not to do. Besides, I believe it can be very counterproductive. It may not be the alleged medium but rather the debunker himself who is perceived as dishonest, and he may come across as arrogant, cynical, and manipulative—not heroic as he imagines.

As well, an apparent reproduction of an *effect* does not necessarily mean the *cause* was the same. (For example, I have seen several skeptical demonstrations of "weeping" icons that employed trickery more sophisticated than that used for "real" crying effigies.) Far better, I am convinced, is showing evidence of the actual methods employed, as I did in collaboration with *Dateline NBC*.

Although John Edward was among five "highly skilled mediums" who allegedly fared well on tests of their ability (Schwartz et al. 2001)—. . . he did not claim validation on *Larry King Live*. When King (2001) asked Edward if he thought there would ever be proof of spirit contact, Edward responded by suggesting proof was unattainable, that only belief matters: ". . . I think that to prove it is a personal thing. It is like saying, prove God. If you have a belief system and you have faith, then there is nothing really more than that." But this is an attempt to insulate a position and to evade or shift the burden of proof, which is always on the claimant. As Houdini (1924,

270) emphatically stated, "It is not for us to prove the mediums are dishonest, it is for them to prove that they *are* honest." In my opinion John Edward has already failed that test.

References

1. Chris Ballard, "Oprah of the Other Side," *New York Times Magazine*, July 29, 2001.
2. Greg Barrett, "Can the Living Talk to the Dead?" *USA Today*, August 10, 2001.
3. John Edward, *One Last Time*. New York: Berkley, 1999.
4. ———, *Crossing Over*. San Diego: Jodere, 2001.
5. Walter B. Gibson, *The Original Houdini Scrapbook*. New York: Corwin/Sterling, 1977.
6. William Lindsay Gresham, *Monster Midway*. New York: Rinehart, 1953.
7. Harry Houdini, *A Magician Among the Spirits*. New York: Harper & Brothers, 1924.
8. Ray Hyman, "Cold Reading: How to Convince Strangers That You Know All About Them," *Skeptical Inquirer*, Spring–Summer 1977.
9. Leon Jaroff, "Talking to the Dead," *Time*, March 5, 2001.
10. M. Lamar Keene, *The Psychic Mafia*. Amherst, NY: Prometheus, 1976. Reprint, 1997.
11. Larry King, "Are Psychics for Real?" *Larry King Live*, March 6, 2001.
12. Georgess McHargue, *Facts, Frauds, and Phantasms: A Survey of the Spiritualist Movement*. Garden City, NY: Doubleday, 1972.
13. Ylan Q. Mui, "Bring Me Your Dead," *New York Post: TV Sunday*, July 8, 2001.
14. Joe Nickell, *Camera Clues*. Lexington: University Press of Kentucky, 1994.
15. ———, "Investigating Spirit Communications," *Skeptical Briefs*. September 1998.
16. ———, "The Davenport Brothers: Religious Practitioners, Entertainers, or Frauds?" *Skeptical Inquirer*, July–August 1999.
17. ———, "Hustling Heaven," *Skeptical Briefs*, September 2000.
18. Joe Nickell, with John F. Fischer, *Secrets of the Supernatural*. Buffalo, NY: Prometheus, 1988.
19. Charles Nordlander, "Letter from Executive Producer of *Crossing Over* to *Time*," March 26, 2001.
20. Gary E.R. Schwartz et al., "Accuracy and Replicability of Anomalous After-Death Communication Across Highly Skilled Mediums," *Journal of the Society for Psychical Research*, January 2001.

Proof of Mediums' Abilities Is Flawed

Richard Wiseman and Ciaran O'Keefe

In the following article, two British writers from Great Britain's University of Hertfordshire's Department of Psychology make the case that after-death communication with mediums is not possible.

Richard Wiseman and Ciaran O'Keefe claim that a highly touted study of famous mediums proves only that human psychology plays a large part in so-called after-death communication and that the outcome of the study was swayed by judging bias, an inappropriate control group, and possibly "sensory leakage," which means the mediums may have gathered information prior to the experiments. The authors' claims are not new; skeptics have been making these very claims for more than a century. Wiseman and O'Keefe conclude that no evidence exists that mediums are contacting the dead.

[G]ary] Schwartz, [Linda] Russek, [Lonnie] Nelson, and [Christopher] Barentsen (2001) [researchers from the Human Energy System Laboratory in Arizona] reported two studies in which mediums appeared to be able to produce accurate information about the deceased under conditions that the [studies'] authors believed "eliminate the factors of fraud, error, and statistical coincidence." Their studies were widely reported in the media as scientific proof of life after death (e.g., Matthews 2001; Chapman 2001). This paper describes some of the methodological problems associated with the Schwartz et al. studies and outlines how these problems can be overcome in future research.

Richard Wiseman and Ciaran O'Keefe, "A Critique of Schwartz et al.'s After-Death Communication Studies," *Skeptical Inquirer*, November–December 2001, pp. 26–30. Copyright © 2001 Committee for the Scientific Investigation of Claims of the Paranormal. Reproduced by permission.

How the Experiment Worked

Schwartz et al.'s first experiment was funded and filmed by a major U.S. television network (Home Box Office—HBO) making a documentary about the survival of bodily death. The study involved two participants (referred to as "sitters") and five well-known mediums. The first sitter was a forty-six-year-old woman who had experienced the death of over six people in the last ten years. Schwartz et al. stated that this sitter was recommended to them by a well-known researcher in ADCs (After Death Communication) who "knew of the sitter's case through her research involving spontaneous ADCs." The second sitter was a fifty-four-year-old woman who had also experienced the death of at least six people in the last ten years.

During the experiment, the sitter and medium sat on either side of a large opaque screen. The medium was allowed to "conduct the reading in his or her own way, with the restriction that they could ask only questions requiring a yes or no answer." Each sitter was asked to listen to the reading and respond to the medium's questions by saying the word "yes" or "no" out loud. The first sitter was given a reading by all five mediums; the second sitter received readings from only two of the mediums.

A few months after the experiment, both sitters were asked to assign a number between -3 (definitely an error) to $+3$ (definitely correct) to each of the statements made by the mediums. The sitters placed 83 percent and 77 percent of the statements into the $+3$ category. Schwartz et al. also reported their attempt to discover whether "intelligent and motivated persons" could guess the type of information presented by the mediums by chance alone. The investigators selected seventy statements from the readings given to the first sitter and turned them into questions. For example, if the medium had said "your father loved dancing," the question became "Who loved to dance?" Sixty-eight undergraduates were shown these questions, along with a photograph of the sitter, and asked to guess the answer. Schwartz et al. reported that the average number of items guessed correctly was just 36 percent, and argue that the high level of accuracy obtained by the mediums could not be due to chance guessing.

The first sitter was then invited back to the laboratory to take part in a second experiment. In this experiment she received readings from two of the mediums who also participated in the first study. Rather than being separated by an opaque screen, the sitter sat six feet behind the medium. In the first part of these two readings the sitter was instructed to remain completely silent. In the second part she was asked to answer "yes" or "no" to each of the medium's questions. After reviewing the readings, the sitter rated 82 percent of the mediums' statements as being "definitely correct."

Three Problems

The Schwartz et al. studies suffered from severe methodological problems, namely: (1) the potential for judging bias, (2) the use of an inappropriate control group, and (3) inadequate safeguards against sensory leakage. Each of these problems will be discussed in turn.

Judging Bias and Selective Remembering

During a mediumistic reading the medium usually produces a large number of statements and the sitter has to decide whether these statements accurately describe his/her deceased friends or relatives. It is widely recognized that the sitter's endorsement of such statements cannot be taken as evidence of mediumistic ability, as seemingly accurate readings can be created by a set of psychological stratagems collectively referred to as "cold reading" (Hyman 1977; Rowland 1998). It is therefore vital that any investigation into the possible existence of mediumistic ability controls for the potential effect of these stratagems. Unfortunately, the Schwartz et al. study did not contain such controls, and thus it is possible that the seemingly impressive results could have been due to cold reading.

Schwartz et al. reproduced a small part of one reading in their paper, and this transcript can be used to illustrate how cold reading could account for the outcome of the studies. In the first line of the transcript the medium said, "Now, I don't know if they [the spirits] mean this by age or by generation, but they talk about the younger male that has passed. Does that make sense to you?" The sitter answered "yes." The medium's statement is ambiguous and open to several different interpretations. When the medium mentioned the word "younger" he/she could be talking about a young child, a young man, or even someone who died young (e.g., in their forties). The sitters may be motivated to interpret such statements in such a way as to maximize the degree of correspondence with their deceased friends and relatives if, for example, they had a strong belief in the afterlife, a need to believe that loved ones have survived bodily death, or were eager to please the mediums, investigators, and the HBO film crew.

In addition, the sitters may have endorsed the readings because some statements caused them to selectively remember certain events in their lives. As a hypothetical example, let us imagine that the medium had said, "Your son was an extrovert." This statement may have caused the sitter to selectively recall certain life events (i.e., the times that her son went to parties and was very outgoing), forget other events (e.g., the times that he sat alone and didn't want to be with others), and thus assign a spuriously high accuracy rating to the statement.

Biased interpretation of ambiguous statements and selective remembering can lead to sitters endorsing contradictory statements during a reading. Interestingly, the short transcript reproduced by Schwartz et al. contains an example of exactly this happening:

Medium: ... your dad speaks about the loss of child. That makes sense?

Sitter: Yes.

Medium: Twice? 'Cause your father says twice.

Sitter: Yes.

Medium: Wait a minute, now he says thrice. He's saying three times. Does that make sense?

Sitter: That's correct.

Some of the statements made by the mediums may also have been true of a great many people and thus had a high likelihood of being endorsed by the sitters. For example, in the transcript the medium stated that one of the spirits was a family member, and elsewhere Schwartz et al. stated that the mediums referred to "a little dog playing ball." It is highly probable that many sitters would have endorsed both of these statements. Research has also revealed that many statements that do not appear especially general can also be true of a surprisingly large number of people. Blackmore (1994) carried out a large-scale survey in which more than 6,000 people were asked to state whether quite specific statements were true of them. More than one third of people endorsed the statement, "I have a scar on my left knee" and more than a quarter answered yes to the statement "Someone in my family is called Jack." In short, the mediums in the Schwartz et al. study may have been accurate, in part, because they simply produced statements that would have been endorsed by many sitters.

Other factors may also increase the likelihood of the sitter endorsing the mediums' statements. Clearly, the more deceased people known to the sitter, the greater chance they will have of being able to find a match for the medium's comments. Both sitters knew a relatively large number of deceased people. Both of them had experienced the death of six loved ones in the last ten years, and the first sitter reported that she believed that the mediums had contacted an additional nine of her deceased friends and relatives. Thus, the sitters' high levels of endorsement may have been due, in part, to them having a large number of deceased friends and relatives.

Inappropriate Control Group Experiment

Schwartz et al. attempted to discover whether the seemingly high accuracy rate obtained by the mediums could have been the result of chance guesswork. However, the method developed by the investigators was inappropriate and fails to address the concerns outlined above. They selected seventy statements from the readings given to the first sitter in the first experiment and turned them into questions. For example, if the medium had said "your son is very good with his hands," the question became "who was very good with his hands?" These questions were presented to a group of undergraduates, who were asked to guess the answers. Schwartz et al. reported that the average number of items guessed correctly was just 36 percent. However, it is extremely problematic to draw any conclusions from this result due to the huge differences in the tasks given to the mediums and control group. For example, when the medium said, "your son was very good with his hands," the sitter has to decide whether this statement matches the information that she knew about her deceased son. However, as noted above, this matching process may be biased by several factors, including her selective remembering and the biased interpretation of ambiguous statements. For example, the sitter may think back to the times that her son built model airplanes, endorse the statement, and the medium would receive a "hit." However, the control group were presented with a completely different task. They were presented with the question "Who was good with his hands?" and would only receive a "hit" if they guessed that the answer was the sitter's son. They therefore had a significantly reduced likelihood of obtaining a hit than the mediums.

Conceptually, this is equivalent to testing archery skills by having someone fire an arrow, drawing a target around wherever it lands and calling it a bullseye, and then testing a "control" group of other archers by asking them to hit the same bullseye. Clearly, the control group would not perform as well as the first archer, but the difference in performance would reflect the fact that they were presented with very different tasks, rather than a difference in their archery skills.

Psychical researchers have developed various methods to overcome the problems associated with "cold reading" when investigating claims of mediumistic ability (see Schouten 1994 for an overview). Most of these methods involve the concept of "blind judging." In a typical experiment, a small number of sitters receive a reading from a medium. The sitters are then asked to evaluate both his or her own reading (often referred to as the "target" reading) and the readings made for other sitters (referred to as "decoy" readings). If the medium is accurate then the ratings assigned to the target readings will be significantly greater than those assigned to the decoy readings. However, it is absolutely vital that the readings are judged "blind"—the sitters should be unaware of whether they are evaluating a "target" or "decoy" reading. This simple safeguard helps overcome all of the problems outlined above. Let us suppose that the medium is not in contact with the spirit world, but instead tends to use cold reading to produce seemingly accurate statements. These techniques will cause the sitters to endorse both the target and decoy readings, and thus produce no evidence for mediumistic ability. If, however, the medium is actually able to communicate with the spirits, the sitters should assign a higher rating to their "target" reading than [to] the "decoy" readings, thus providing evidence of mediumistic ability.

It is hoped that future tests of mediumistic ability will employ the type of blind judging methods that have been developed, and frequently employed, in past tests of mediumistic ability.

However, blind judging is only one of several methodological safeguards that should be employed when testing mediumistic ability. Well-controlled tests should also obviously prevent the medium from being able to receive information about a sitter through any normal channels of communication. Unfortunately, the measures taken by Schwartz et al. to guard against various forms of potential sensory leakage appear insufficient.

Weak Safeguards Against Sensory Leakage

Throughout all of the readings in the first experiment, and the latter part of the readings in the second experiment, the sitter was allowed to answer "yes" or "no" to the medium's questions. These answers would have provided the mediums with two types of information that may have helped them produce more accurate statements in the remainder of the reading. First, it is very likely that the sitter's voice would have given away clues about her gender, age, and socioeconomic group. This information could cause the mediums to produce statements that have a greater likelihood of being endorsed by the sitter. For example, an older sitter is more likely to have experienced the death of their parents than a younger sitter, and certain life events are gender-specific (e.g., being pregnant, having a miscarriage, etc.). Second, the sitters' answers may have also given away other useful clues to the mediums. For example, let us imagine that the medium stated, "I am getting the impression of someone male, is that correct?" If the sitter has recently lost someone very close to her, such as a father or son, then she might answer a tearful "yes." If, however, the deceased male was an uncle that sitter didn't really know very well, then her "yes" might be far less emotional. Again, a skilled medium might be able to unconsciously use this information to produce accurate statements later in the reading. Any well-controlled test of mediumistic ability should not allow for the sitter to provide verbal feedback to the medium during the reading.

In the first part of the readings in the second experiment, the sitter was asked not to answer yes or no to any of the medium's statements. However, the experimental set-up still employed insufficient safeguards against potential sensory leakage. The medium sat facing a video camera and the sitter sat six feet behind the medium without any form of screen separating the two of them. As such, the sitter may have emitted various types of sensory signals, such as cues from her movement, breathing, odor, etc. Parapsychologists have developed elaborate procedures for eliminating potential sensory leakage between participants (e.g., Milton and Wiseman 1997). These safeguards frequently involve placing participants in separate rooms, and often the use of specially constructed sound-attenuated cubicles. Schwartz et al. appeared to have ignored these guidelines and instead allowed the sitter to interact with the medium, and/or simply seated them behind one another in the same room. Neither of these measures represent sufficient safeguards against the potential for sensory leakage.

The investigators also failed to rule out the potential for sensory leakage between the experimenters and mediums. The second sitter in the first experiment is described as being "personally known" to two of the experimenters (Schwartz and Russek). The report also described how, during the experiment, the mediums were allowed to chat with Russek in a courtyard behind the laboratory. Research into the possible existence of mediumistic ability should not allow anyone who knows the sitter to come into contact with the medium. Schwartz allowed such contact, with their only safeguard being that the mediums and Russek were not allowed to talk about matters related to the session. However, a large body of research has shown that there are many ways in which information can be unwittingly communicated, via both verbal and nonverbal means (e.g., Rosenthal and Rubin 1978). As such, the safeguards employed by Schwartz et al. against possible sensory leakage between experimenter and mediums were insufficient.

In short, the Schwartz et al. study did not employ blind judging, employed an inappropriate control group, and had insufficient safeguards against sensory leakage. As such, it is impossible to know the degree to which their findings represent evidence for mediumistic ability. Psychical researchers have worked hard to develop robust methods for testing mediums since the 1930s (see Schouten 1994). It is hoped that future work in this area will build upon the methodological guidelines that have been developed and thus minimize the type of problems discussed here.

References

1. S. Blackmore, "Probability Misjudgement and Belief in the Paranormal: Is the Theory All Wrong?" In D. Bierman ed., *Proceedings of the 37th Annual Convention of the Parapsychological Association*, 1994.
2. J. Chapman, "Is There Anybody There? Mediums Perform Well in Scientific Séance Test," *Daily Mail* [London], March 5, 2001.
3. R. Hyman, "Cold Reading: How to Convince Strangers That You Know All About Them," *Skeptical Inquirer*, 1977.
4. R. Matthews, "Spiritualists' Powers Turn Scientists into Believers," *Sunday Telegraph* [London], March 4. 2001.
5. J. Milton and R. Wiseman, *Guidelines for Extrasensory Perception Research*. Hatfield, UK: University of Hertfordshire Press, 1997.
6. R. Rosenthal and D.B. Rubin, "Interpersonal Expectancy Effects: The First 345 Studies," *Behavioural and Brain Sciences*, no. 3, 1978.
7. I. Rowland, *The Full Facts Book of Cold Reading*. London: Ian Roland, 1998.
8. S.A. Schouten, "An Overview of Quantitatively Evaluated Studies with Mediums and Psychics," *Journal of the American Society for Psychical Research*, 1994.
9. G.E.R. Schwartz (et al.), "Accuracy and Replicability of Anomalous After-Death Communication Across Highly Skilled Mediums," *Journal of the Society for Psychical Research*, 2001.

Television Mediums Are Not Authentic

James Underdown

From the late 1990s until 2004, television featured popular shows with mediums contacting the deceased loved ones of members of the audience. The two most talked-about shows were Beyond, *hosted by James Van Praagh, and* Crossing Over, *hosted by John Edward. While loyal fans watched the shows with unquestioning devotion, skeptics had immediate concerns.*

James Underdown reports in this article the findings of a group of skeptics who attended these shows. Prior to attending a taping of Van Praagh's Beyond, *the undercover attendees were called by producers and questioned. This raised the skeptics' suspicions that Van Praagh researched the audience before pretending to communicate with the deceased. During the show, the undercover skeptics observed him talking to an audience member before the show, and only then was he able to give an "accurate" reading while the cameras rolled.*

Underdown attended a taping of John Edward's Crossing Over. *At first he did not see anything suspicious, nor anything suggesting real ability. Later he compared what actually happened to the final, edited versions of a few shows. He found that inaccurate statements that Edward had made were cut.*

The undercover skeptics were part of the Independent Investigations Group (IIG). IIG members are also members of the Center for Inquiry-West, which is the West Coast headquarters for the Committee for the Scientific Investigation of Claims of the Paranormal, which in turn publishes Skeptical Inquirer, *where this article appeared. James Underdown is the executive director of the Center for Inquiry-West.*

James Underdown, "They See Dead People—or Do They? An Investigation of Television Mediums," *Skeptical Inquirer*, September–October 2003, pp. 41–44. Copyright © 2003 Committee for the Scientific Investigation of Claims of the Paranormal. Reproduced by permission.

John Edward MaGee Jr. (known as John Edward) and James Van Praagh are probably the two most famous mediums in the United States today. Their shows *Crossing Over* and *Beyond*, respectively, were both running in the fall and winter of 2002–2003. Both syndicated shows had their host speaking with (or "reading") audiences (or "sitters") and claiming to make connections with the deceased friends and/or family of the audience members. Some of the shows featured readings of celebrities or individuals with special stories to tell.

Both mediums enjoy considerable success. Van Praagh sells lots of books and has a number of celebrities as clients. Edward, also, hawks books, and [started his television career in] June of 2000. Both men [played] to large audiences around the country. Even *Skeptical Inquirer* has included articles about them.[1] . . .

When Van Praagh started taping *Beyond* a few blocks from the Center for Inquiry-West [CFI-West] in Hollywood, our homegrown Independent Investigations Group (IIG) sprang into action. (The IIG consists of a dedicated group of inquirers who participate with CFI-West staff in hands-on investigations.)

Even some skeptics seemed to be impressed with the mediums' on-camera abilities, and speculated about why they seemed so successful. Were they getting "hot reads" (using information gotten prior to the taping) through audience microphones, audience plants, or through production research? Was there some trick we weren't aware of helping these two look so accurate? Would the tapings we witnessed differ from the fully edited, aired shows? We attempted to find out.

Undercover at a Live Taping

Several IIG members attended two [of Van Praagh's] *Beyond* tapings, descending in groups of seven or eight to the studio after a briefing at CFI-West. We split up into smaller groups with our well-hidden recording gear, and went to work.

Before the actual tape date, a number of us who had requested tickets received phone calls from Van Praagh's production people asking who we wanted to contact and what our story was. These calls seemed to be searching for candidates for the more intense, one-on-one readings Van Praagh included in each show.

On the day of the tapings, we split up in order to have a better chance of spotting plants in line as the audience waited outside the studio. We all signed fake names on the voluminous release form . . . , and engaged in conversations about fictitious friends and relatives. If any of these stories made their way into a reading, we'd know the information had been obtained somewhere in or near the studio.

Upon entering the studio, we noticed standard audience microphones hanging from the ceiling, and speakers placed along the floors. We also monitored both Van Praagh's and his warm-up woman's pre-show conversations. That proved to be interesting.

While phone-interviewing audience members might be a conduit of information to Van Praagh, it's also consistent with the best interest of the producer trying to find compelling content. Indeed, Van Praagh's in-studio readings were so unimpressive that our suspicions of hot reading were lowered. If he had his researchers gleaning spicy tidbits for his readings, they weren't doing a very good job, for he often struggled in his efforts.

Some of the remote one-on-one segments were more impressive, but those generally took place in the sitter's homes where many clues to his or her life might be noticeable. We don't know if producers leaked information to Van Praagh or not, and we never saw raw footage of what went on at the remote tapings. Editing, as I will discuss later, could have played a crucial role.

We saw no evidence of spies in line trying to draw information from people. We gave no information beyond the contact data on the release form. None of our fake names or stories turned up in readings. Before Van Praagh's taping began, loud music was played which would have made it extremely difficult to hear a conversation from the audience microphones.

Van Praagh was guilty of at least one cheat that could be considered a hot read. Before tape was rolling, he signed some books and was chatting with members of the audience. He learned during one conversation that a woman in the audience was from Italy. When the cameras were rolling, he asked who in that section was from another country. If one hadn't seen the earlier conversation, the woman raising her hand in the affirmative would have been impressive, when in fact he knew quite well what the response would be.

Nothing Suspicious, at First

I attended a taping of John Edward's *Crossing Over* in Queens, New York, alone in November of 2002. *Crossing Over* looked like a production that had a few years under its belt. There was a waiting room instead of a long line outside, the security was a little better (I had to show a real I.D.), and they seemed to run a much tighter ship, though I did get my pocket-sized digital recorder inside with no problem.

Again, there were no indications of anyone I saw collecting information. Edward, too, played music fairly loudly, making it tough to hear normal conversation. And again, none of his readings contained the kind of specific information that would raise an eyebrow of suspicion. In fact, during most of the show I witnessed, John Edward was a bad cold reader. He, too, struggled to get hits, and in one attempt shot off nearly forty guesses before finding any significant targets. . . .

Cold reading, in a nutshell, is an interactive technique where one fishes for information while giving the appearance of receiving that information from supernatural sources. Both of these men rattle off gobs of guesses until they find a vein of hits with one of their audience members. They are very adept at steering out of dead ends and helping the crowd forgive and forget their mistakes.

Why Cold Reading Appears Impressive

In the context of a studio audience full of people, cold reading is not very impressive. Consider that the audience at each of the tapings we witnessed consisted of about 200 people, in three sections of sixty-to-seventy each. If the average person's address book holds about 150 people[2] (mine has well over 300), we can probably be safe in presuming that we actually *know* many more people than those whose numbers we have. But let's use the 150 figure as a very conservative estimate of an active database from which most people have to draw.

This means that when John Edward or James Van Praagh asks a section of his audience, "Who's Margaret?" he is hoping there is a Margaret in the 10,000 people in the database of that section. If there is no answer, they open the question up to the whole audience's database of over 30,000 people! Would it be surprising for there to be a dozen Margarets in such a large sample?

I submit that these databases are so large that they explain the occasional amazing-sounding home run of a hit. I saw John Edward swinging for the fence by asking who died from getting hit by lightning. When no one answered even after he amended the guess to mere electrocution, he remarked that you'd think you'd remember if you knew someone who passed from something like that.

Let's not forget that when a medium initiates a conversation with an audience member or group of members, he enjoys the benefit of visually appraising whomever he's speaking with. When conversing with a group of ladies over sixty, Edward guessed the names Helen and Margaret as the peers and parents of the women, not Tiffany or Courtney, names more likely to be given to younger people. Any good cold reader uses visual clues to refine his guessing.

Audience Preparation Improves the Performance

Both shows went through a lot of effort to get their audiences in the right frame of mind before taping. People came to the tapings to contact a dead loved one. The *Crossing Over* instructions put it bluntly. "If you feel you will be too embarrassed, too frazzled, or just not interested, we ask that you give up your seat to someone who is anxious for a reading."

The audience was admonished not to expect to be read, and that some things the host would say would make sense, others wouldn't. Much of the pre-show rhetoric seemed to be aimed at keeping our expectations low. Both men were very self-effacing, charming, and good-humored, endearing themselves to the audience.

The eight-page letter Edward sent out to his audience included sections entitled "Information For A Positive Session" and "Recommended Things To Think About." The latter began with the subsection "Know your entire family tree." He reminds us to remember dates, to visualize spouse's families, estranged family, and stepfamilies—even pets. Your personal database, after all, is only as good as your ability to recall it.

After a rather New Agey, meditative preface, Van Praagh's warm-up person was emphatic about reacting openly to what James was saying. How's he supposed to know if he's on the right track? she might as well have said.

Questioning the Fine Print

Anyone attending either *Crossing Over* or *Beyond* had to sign a four-page appearance release. (Standard releases are one page.) Edward's release had the feel of a document written by someone just accused of cheating. It seemed to focus on representing that attendees had no outside contact with Edward or his staff, or in documenting that fact if they had. This tone was reinforced vigorously in the studio where we were reminded constantly not to talk about ourselves or those who we were trying to contact. It was as if the specter of Harry Houdini were floating above the stage pointing a finger.

Van Praagh's release—also four pages—included a nondisclosure section that reads in part: "Neither anyone acting on my behalf, nor I . . . shall speak to any newspaper reporter, print or television journalist or other media representative or source about any aspect of my participation in the Series. . . ."

Editing Highlights the Hits, Downplays the Misses

We decided that the best way to see if any editing wizardry was taking place on these shows was to record segments of the live taping and compare those to the edited versions America saw on the air. What we found was one of the keys to the TV psychic kingdom.

I have some experience sitting in an editing room trying to turn large amounts of raw videotape into small amounts of polished gold. So I know that virtually everything you see on TV has been precisely edited for both time and content. We cannot indict these programs for editing the footage recorded in the studios, but it should be understood that the aired tape does not represent how the readings went in the studio. The aired versions of these programs show a much more successful account of the readings. Here are two examples.

This is what aired . . .

Van Praagh: You were saved by someone. A car thing, or something where you were . . .

Woman: We actually had a car accident four months after my husband died. And we were in a very bad collision.

Van Praagh: You almost died, honey. Because I'm being told by your husband that you were saved, Ok?

This is what happened. . .

Van Praagh: You almost died, honey. Because I'm being told by your husband that you were spared, you were saved, Ok? You were saved, all right? And I know [here, Van Praagh is saying, "I know" to some unseen voice or spirit] . . . something about Jesus here, Ok? Saved with Jesus, or something about Jesus, and if you believe in Jesus, or a religious element. And I don't know, maybe a church with the name Jesus in it? Or there is something about Jesus. Or there's . . .

Woman (interrupting): Well, we're Jewish! (Big laugh from the audience.)

John Edward's editor fine-tuned many of the dead-ends out of a reading riddled with misses. Here, the italicized parts never made it to air.

Edward: Ok, just so you know in my reference, how I got it was a funny thing. So whatever race you went to go see, that you had taped, something funny happened at it, because I would have thought you went to a comedy show. Ok. *Just so you know that you viewed it, he viewed it as a funny thing. Ok. Now the twenty-sixth is significant your grounding birthday anniversary but there's a twenty-sixth connection. I also feel like I don't know if . . .* I think there's a Michael that's passed as well. I know your Michael's [to the woman] here, but I've got a Michael who's passed who's connected here as well. And I think he either had cerebral palsy, or he had like a neural muscular disease.

It's a name like Michael or Mark, Mick, an "M" name I feel like he like cerebral palsy, he had something like spina bifida— there's like that kind of a feeling. Are you sure it's not for you? That's not for you? . . .

Man: No

Edward: Positive?

Man: Positive.

Edward: He's with you or behind you, but he's right here.

Who would have like a penny or a like coin that's like laminated or saved?

Woman: I would.

Edward: Then this is for you guys. So somehow you guys are connected to this kid. Or to this—it might not have been a kid, but he feels like he's a kid to me. There's an "M."

We saw James Van Praagh stop tape during a one-on-one, prearranged reading after missing all but one of his first six or seven guesses. He then restarted the tape and used the one correct guess at the beginning of the new session. I think most people would call that cheating. Skeptics and television viewers everywhere should be mindful that a good editor can make a pitcher bat a thousand, magician David Blaine levitate above a sidewalk, and a former dance instructor sound like he's conversing with dead people.

Conclusion: Television Mediums Are Fakes

Television psychics generally have a pretty good recipe for appearing to possess paranormal ability. Large audiences gobble up these unreality shows like popcorn.

Skeptics have been served these hot and cold reading techniques for ages, and we saw nothing new or surprising in their methods. The "hit" rate we witnessed for both John Edward and James Van Praagh was disappointing at best. But the fat got "cleaned up in post" (production), as they say in Hollywood.

The mixture of a well-prepared and uncritical audience made it easy to create an atmosphere of cooperation and success in the studio. Strict appearance releases and competent editing made it easy to keep the lid on mistakes and make the medium seem impressive.

Update

Apparently, Hollywood wasn't big enough for both men; mega-distributor Tribune Media Services dropped James Van Praagh in January 2003. [John Edward's show was canceled in 2004.]

Notes

1. Joe Nickell, "Speaking to the Dead," *Skeptical Inquirer*, November/December 2001. Also, Ray Hyman's "How *Not* to Test Mediums," *Skeptical Inquirer*, January–February 2003.
2. Matt Ridley, *The Origins of Virtue*. New York: Viking Penguin 1996.

Mediums Are Skilled Speakers

Robin Wooffitt

Robin Wooffitt studies verbal patterns, such as pauses, repetitions, volume, inflection, stumbling, and clarity. Wooffitt analyzed mediums' speech to attempt to gain an understanding of how mediums do what they do.

First, Wooffitt found that mediums rely on "reported speech" —that is, they will claim to repeat something that a spirit has, supposedly, just spoken to them. Mediums report the exact words the spirit is saying. This is a tactic that can seem very impressive to the sitter. In turn, the medium establishes credibility.

Second, Wooffitt observes that mediums use the present tense of verbs, which makes it sound like the spirit is present, listening, and watching. Again, the idea of an immediate spirit is essential if a medium is going to have a positive session with a sitter.

Wooffitt also discusses how silence is problematic for mediums and how mediums sidestep awkward moments when they give mistaken information. He concludes that mediums are using a form of institutional discourse. This means that organization and sequence are keys—what is being said is not as credible as how it is being said, but most audiences don't pay attention to these dynamics. Instead, they are wowed by what appears to be human-spirit communication.

Wooffitt teaches at the University of York in the United Kingdom. He has published five books on discourse. His latest book is The Language of Mediums and Psychics: The Social Organisation of Everyday Miracles.

This article reports a study of the use of reported speech in interaction between members of the public and mediums: people who say that they are able to communicate with the dead on behalf of the living.[1]

The very notion of mediumship embodies a series of fantastically controversial claims: that some aspect of the human personality survives death: that spirits can monitor the ongoing lives of those they left behind; and that it is possible for some people to establish a parapsychological link with the spirit world so that they can pass on messages to the living. It is no surprise that there is a distinct polarization in lay and academic attitudes towards the authenticity of mediumship in general, and the evidential value of mediums' discourse in particular.

Sceptics and some academic psychologists treat mediums' discourse suspiciously, regarding it as the site of deliberate and exploitative fraud, or at best, a collaborative exercise in self-delusion by well-intentioned but credulous individuals. The anecdotal evidence offered by believers is explained away as a consequence of cold reading, a set of interpretative, observational and linguistic practices by which people without any special powers can produce what may be interpreted as a convincing demonstration of paranormal cognition: especially if the client or sitter is predisposed to believe in the paranormal, or has some deep-rooted wish to be presented with evidence of the spiritual existence of a particular individual such as a spouse, parent or child (Christopher, 1970, 1975: Hyman, 1981: Randi, 1981; Roe, 1995). Yet for many, the medium's reports of spirit messages will be interpreted fairly unquestioningly as direct evidence for spirit existence, and in support of the medium's claims to be able to communicate with the spirit world (for example, Best, 1991; Ellison, 1988; Keen et al., 1999, and any issue of *Psychic News*, the weekly newspaper for mediums and other psychic practitioners).

What is crucial though, is that the medium establishes his or her powers, and by implication, the existence of the spirit world, to the satisfaction of the client, or sitter. This may be accomplished by relaying intimate or private information about the sitter provided by the medium's spirit contacts. Al-

ternatively the spirits may use the medium to present various
kinds of advice to the sitter.

Using Reported Speech

One intuitively arresting way of demonstrating the presence of
the spirits is to report the words spoken by the spirit to the
medium. This is a common occurrence in medium-sitter interaction. In the following extract, for example, the medium is
reporting the spirit's characterization of how she felt at the
time of her death.

[**Extract 1**] ('M' is the medium, 'S' is the sitter or client.)[2]

   M: she said I was so

   S: yes

   M: tired.

   M: I didn't [want to] eat[;] I didn't want to do anything.

   M: I just was tired.

   S: mm hm

And in Extract 2 the medium uses direct reported speech to
reveal what the spirit (referred to as 'he') said about the sitter.

[**Extract 2**]

   M: he says she can be quite stubborn at times y'know.

   M: is that true?

   S1: yes

Mediums thus may introduce the spirits' very words into the
sitting as a way of presenting knowledge claims about the sitter as evidence of post-mortem survival of some form of conscious spirit entity. As such, these instances of reported speech
may be examined as a discursive practice which meets perhaps

the key requirement of mediumship: demonstrations of the sentient, co-present dead.

In recent years there have been a number of studies of the use of reported speech in a variety of settings and discursive contexts: in everyday interaction (Holt, 1996; Mayes, 1990; Tannen, 1986); in courtroom interaction (Phillips, 1986); in group discussions (Buttny, 1998; Buttny and Williams, 2000; Myers, 1999); in political discussion (Leudar, 1998) and in accounts of anomalous or paranormal experiences (Wooffitt, 1992). Many of these studies depart from the more linguistic and grammatical concerns with reported speech (for example, Coulmas, 1986; Li, 1986) and the exploration of its more psychological or cognitive aspects (Lehrer, 1989), and have instead begun to investigate more sociological questions which are raised when people incorporate another's utterances into ongoing encounters.

Goffman's (1981) discussion of footing established and subsequently framed much of the more sociologically oriented work on reported speech. Specifically, he [wanted] to provide a more sophisticated treatment of the status of participants than that offered by their characterization as speaker and hearer. To this end, he examined the various 'production formats' by which speakers may position themselves in relation to their own utterances, or with respect to the utterances of others. He proposed an analytic distinction between 'animator' (the person actually speaking), 'author' (the person who originally formulated the opinions or ideas being expressed) and 'principal' (whose perspective or viewpoint is displayed in the current turn), thus providing the conceptual resources by which to track the fluidity of involvement in discourse.

How Mediums Speak Is Unique

It would appear that medium-sitter interaction invites an investigation of footing shifts for two reasons. First, during a sitting there are, ostensibly, three parties to the interaction, but with different communicative capabilities and responsibilities. The medium can communicate with two parties, the living and the dead; the spirit can communicate to the medium directly, but to the sitter only through the medium; and although rare in the present corpus, it would be possible for the sitter to attempt to communicate directly with the spirit (for example, by asking questions) or via the medium (by asking the medium to ask the spirit a question). The very nature of the event, then, requires that the medium speak for the spirit, and this in turn invites footing shifts.[3]

Second, there is the issue of scepticism. Mediums are providing a service which requires the demonstration of magical abilities which in turn requires the existence and participation of a class of entities whose . . . [existence] is, at the very least, controversial. Even if the sitters are utterly convinced of the afterlife, and the possibility of communication with its denizens, any particular sitting occurs within a wider, sceptical cultural frame of reference (see also Wooffitt, 1992). This means that mediums have to address the possibility that the authenticity of their claims may be called into question. They have to demonstrate that the information they provide really does come from a paranormal source, and is not simply gleaned from observation of the sitters, or a reformulation of information inadvertently provided by the sitters. One way in which this can be achieved is to establish that the source of information which has been accepted or confirmed by the sitter has come from a source which is patently independent of the medium. And, clearly, reporting the spirit's own words is a crucial resource by which this may be accomplished in the course of the sitting. The presentation of an utterance as coming from a spirit source entails that the medium is presenting him or herself as, in Goffman's (1981) terms, the animator rather than the author of the utterance. Footing shifts may thus provide for the sense of an independent spirit entity disclosing information to the medium which is then hinted at or implied in the medium's questions to or statements about the sitter.

However, Goffman's approach raises methodological problems. . . . His studies of language use do not systematically explore the significance of the sequential organization of interaction, the examination of which is at the heart of conversation analytic (CA) studies (Schegloff, 1988; see also Clayman, 1992). As this article is at least partly concerned with the location of reported speech in robust patterns of turn taking, the subsequent discussion [will look at] . . . sequence, interaction and inference.

Knowing What a Spirit Is Actually Saying

For example: Holt (1996) examined conversational instances of direct reported speech, in which the current speaker reproduces the words of another person in such a way as to suggest that this is what was actually said at the time. She reports a number of interactional functions of direct reported speech. For example, reported speech permits the speaker to demonstrate an assessment of the person whose talk is being reported in the way their words are reproduced. It allows the speaker to display what he or she considers to be, for example, the relevant attitudes, opinions, personality traits, or general state of mind of the person whose talk they are reporting at the time it was originally produced. But more relevant to the concerns of this article, it provides a key resource by which speakers can provide evidence for a position, or attest to the factuality of a claim or version of events (Potter, 1996).

This sociological perspective on the interactional organization of reported speech liberates analytic focus from whether or not the medium's claimed powers are true, and invites a series of empirically investigable questions about medium-sitter interaction which should be of interest both to those who are sceptical and those for whom it offers glimpses into the afterlife. For example: *when* do mediums choose to report the words of the spirits? Are there particular kinds of discursive contexts which seem to lend themselves to the reproduction of the spirit's words? What are the design characteristics of spirit utterances? Moreover, *what* do the spirits say? And what do their words *do*? That is, what kinds of actions do the reports of those utterances perform in the context of the sitting? In short, what is the social organization and function of reported speech in the interactional production of the co-present dead?

Mediums Follow a Three-Step Pattern

Mediums, along with other sorts of psychic practitioners, claim that they are able to gain knowledge about an individual through paranormal powers. The successful demonstration of these special powers exhibit some robust properties. In sittings, psychic practitioners will issue a series of utterances, usually (but not invariably) in the form of questions which hint at or imply, that they have access to knowledge about the sitter or their circumstances. If the sitter finds the psychic's utterance to be accurate, or is in some way relevant, it is receipted and accepted with a minimal turn, usually a simple 'yes' or 'yeah'. After the sitter's minimal acceptance or confirmation the psychic practitioner moves swiftly to a turn in which the now-accepted knowledge is attributed to a paranormal source. . . .

There is, then, a three-turn sequence [referred to as T1, T2, and T3] which is a vehicle for demonstrations of ostensibly paranormal cognition:

T1 question (or statement) implying or hinting at knowledge of the sitter;

T2 minimal acceptance by the sitter;

T3 attribution of now-accepted knowledge to a paranormal source.

In this sequence the third turn is crucial as it provides a slot in which psychics may establish their paranormal abilities. Moreover, insofar as the sitters' minimal acceptances quickly return the floor to the psychic, and thereby facilitate the early onset of the third turn, they may be said to be displaying an orientation to the significance of the third turn. Consequently, this sequence may be said to be socially organized and collaboratively produced (Wooffitt, 2001).

In medium-sitter interaction, it is noticeable that reports of spirit utterances cluster strongly in attributive third turns of success sequences. In Extract [3] the medium claims to be in contact with the spirit of the sitter's husband, and is describing some of his personality characteristics.

[**Extract 3**]

> M: he's very tough-skinned. and it feels like he doesn't let many people through, but he let you through.
>
> S: mm hm
>
> M: you understand?
>
> S: yes.
>
> M: and this is what he is talking about.
>
> S: [Okay.]
>
> M: he said he let Liz through. Did he ever call you Lizzie?
>
> S: Yes
>
> M: because he says "I let Lizzie through."
>
> S: mm hm

Here the first turn in the sequence, the question "did he ever call you Lizzie?" receives a positive response from the sitter. The medium then reports the spirit's utterance: 'I let Lizzie through'! ... The medium's third turn begins with 'because'. This provides for an understanding as to how the psychic knew that 'Lizzie' might have been a name used by the sitter's husband when he was alive: the spirit was using it there and then in his interaction with the medium.

Extract [4] comes from the early part of a sitting, and the medium is asking questions to determine whose spirit the sitter is most keen to contact. While many of these initial exploratory questions receive positive answers, the medium does not move to an attributive third turn. This may be because the now accepted information is still too vague to provide for a satisfactory or credible demonstration of paranormal powers. It is only when the sitter confirms the medium's question "is this your husband who passed over please?" that an attributive third turn is produced, and the words of the sitter's dead husband are introduced.

[Extract 4]

M: Does this make sense to you? in your purse or in your bag [could] picture please

S: [Yes]

M: Is this of a man or a male?

S: Yes

M: and isn't that the person you want to contact?

S: Yes

M: hmm He is very strong. I am not sure what [to]

M: is this your husband who passed over please?

S: [Yes]

M: 'cause he just said husband "I'm her husband, I'm her husband" 'kay? good.

In the extracts so far, the spirits' reported utterances provide the sitters with unambiguous evidence that they were the source of the information implied or hinted at in the medium's first turn in the sequence. For example, 'because he says "I let Lizzie through" ' is plainly hearable as the source of the medium's earlier inquiry 'did he ever call you Lizzie?'. However, the spirits' utterances may be reproduced in such a way as to make their attributive status inferentially available. In Extract [5] the claim made in the first-turn position can be inferred to be derived from the spirit world by virtue of what the spirit is reported as saying in response to the sitter's acceptance.

[Extract 5]

> M: [Have you had a bit of] trouble with your back as well.
>
> S1: yes a little bit
>
> M: he says "ah'd [I'd] best send her a bit of sympathy down" so you understand it?
>
> S1: yes

So, even though "ah'd best send her a bit of sympathy down" does not explicitly refer to the sitter's back problem, it is clearly topically relevant; moreover, it is an appropriate response to the sitter's confirmation to the medium 2 she has a health problem. The relevance and appropriateness of the spirit's utterances provide the basis to interpret the presence of the spirit as the original source of the information about the sitter's condition.

Mediums Change Tactics with Large Audiences

The sequential patterning of reported speech is also evident in a related but markedly different context. In private sittings, the medium has to demonstrate his or her powers to the co-present sitter (or sitters, if more than one). Moreover, the demonstrations of the medium's powers are produced for the same sitter(s) on each and every occasion. In larger demonstrations to audiences in a theatre or hall, however, there are some significant differences. First, the recipient or referent of spirit messages changes over the course of the demonstration. Moreover, the attributive third turn has to work as a convincing demonstration not only to the relevant individual, but to the rest of the overhearing audience as well. The following extract comes from a recording of the well-known British medium Doris Stokes demonstrating her mediumistic skills to an audience in a theatre in London.

[Extract 6]

M: Now, there's—somebody up there who's just got a new cooker put in.

S: Yes.

S: (I have.)

M: hhhh Y'know—.

S: That's right. I used it today, Doris, for the first time.

M: You used it today?

S: (*smiling voice*) Yes.

M: And [I've] another voice come, an' she says, 'she's just bought a new cooker you know.' They know—, they get to know everything.

Stokes begins by stating that someone 'up there' (referring, presumably, to the balcony, not to the spirit world) has recently got a new cooker, or oven. A member of the audience confirms this, thus identifying herself as the person to whom Stokes was referring. Stokes then initiates a turn where a third position attribution might occur ('hhhh Y'know—') but abandons her utterances when the sitter speaks again, reaffirming the newness of the cooker by stating that she has only just used it for the first time. Stokes receipts this information, soliciting a further confirmation from the sitter. Stokes then provides the attributive turn, in which an unidentified spirit voice is reproduced to indicate that the knowledge about the cooker came from a spirit source.

There are two observations. First, the sitter's report of the first use of the cooker occurs in the slot in which an attributive turn would be expected. However, the onset of sitter's talk does not lead to the abandonment of the third turn: after responding to the sitter's utterance, Stokes produces the attributive turn, thereby treating the sitter's prior turn as initiating an insertion sequence which merely delayed the onset of the still relevant third turn. Second, the reproduction of the spirit's utterance in the context of a presentation to an audience suggests its robustness and flexibility as an interactional resource for establishing the paranormal origin of now accepted knowledge claims.

Finally in this section, we can consider a textual instance of the use of reported speech in an attributive third turn. This comes from a report of a public demonstration by the British medium Stephen O'Brien, published originally in *The Psychic News*, the weekly newspaper for spiritualists, mediums and psychics. It was reproduced in O'Brien's autobiography.

[**Extract 7**]

'Your great-grandmother is telling me about this', Stephen explained, and she says, 'I'm Mary Jane.'

'Oh yes, that's her name!' answered the delighted recipient.

'She says you're thinking of marrying soon.'

'I am.'

'Mary Jane is telling me "He's a good looking boy. Tell her I approve."'

Regardless of whether the journalist's account is accurate or not, it displays many of the organizational features of routine success sequences. There is a claim to knowledge (that the sitter is getting married), a minimal acceptance or confirmation, and then a spirit's utterance—topically related to the medium's prior turn—is reproduced for the sitter. One key difference here is that the spirit is described as the source of the knowledge in the first turn. Such first position attributions, however, are rare. And even in this case, the attribution to a spirit source of the first position knowledge claim is achieved by *indirect* reported speech. It is not until the third position in this sequence that the spirit's words are reproduced in direct reported speech.

The three-part success sequence which makes use of reported speech in the attributive third turn is one of the key 'fingerprints' (Heritage and Greatbatch. 1991: 95–6) of the collaborative production of agentic, independent spirit entities. Although grounded in face-to-face interaction, it seems to inform not only demonstrations of spirit presence to sitters in an audience, but also the organization of narrative accounts in texts about mediums' successful demonstration of spirit presence.

Its organization clearly orients to socially organized inferential concerns; for example, the absence of attributive components in first-position knowledge claims, and the appearance of spirit utterances after knowledge claims have been ratified by the sitter, minimize the likelihood that the medium is seen as endorsing factually incorrect or irrelevant information. This may be taken as inviting a sceptical interpretation of the validity of the medium's powers. . . . Whether mediums are truly in touch with the spirit world or perpetrating deliberate fraud, the way in which their powers are demonstrated and ratified is socially organized and collaboratively produced. This article is simply concerned to document the methodic properties by which viable presence of the spirit world is discursively produced. . . .

Reporting Direct Speech from a Spirit Engages the Sitter

It has been noted previously that direct reported speech is an extremely effective method by which a speaker can produce an account or narrative which is engaging for the recipient. Reported speech adds immediacy to the narrative, provides for the vividness of the tale and facilitates the recipient's involvement in the account. This is certainly the case in reported speech in medium-sitter interaction. Given that most spirits seem to have some clear significance for the sitter, reported speech presents the sitter with direct evidence not only of the post-mortem survival of their parents or spouse, but indicates the way in which their spirit's co-presence (albeit modulated by the special abilities of the medium) becomes manifest throughout the course of the sitting. Indeed, the spirit's overwhelming concern with the activities of the living or their past life together, establishes that the spirits are capable of being mindful of those they left behind. Moreover, insofar as the spirits can be depicted as responding in real time to the topical trajectory of the exchanges between the sitter and the medium, they too become interactionally relevant. This in turn further enhances the sense of the spirit as an existing entity possessing everyday perceptual and cognitive abilities.

This sense of a co-present cognizing agent is an extremely important feature of the sitting in that it facilitates the sitter's understanding that the spirit entity in contact with the medium is indeed the spirit of the person they knew: the reports of the spirit's words provide the basis upon which a sitter might come to infer a discernible and recognizable personality, biography, and so on.

In the following case, the medium establishes that the sitter's mother has died and then claims that her spirit is present in the room and reproduces her words. This provides for the interpretation that the spirit referred to, prior to the confirmation that the sitter's mother has died, is the same spirit.

[Extract 8]

> M: So spirit wants me to do a scan on your body, talk about your health, so I'm going to do that okay? I'm going to do this for your health. Let's see what's going on with you . . . number one thing, is your mother in spirit please?
>
> S: yes
>
> M: 'cause I have [your] mother standing right over here. and she said "I WANNA TALK to HER and I want to speak to her" because your mother has very loud . . . when she comes through she speaks with a . . . in a very loud way . . . a very, uhm, understand very she has to be
>
> S: [Yes]
>
> M: heard, and like this would not happen today without her coming through for you. [Do you understand?]
>
> S: [Okay]
>
> S: Yes.
>
> M: b'cause she wants to be heard, and that's what she's talking about the first thing I want to talk about is, she's mentioning something about the head area

In this extract the reported speech accomplishes several tasks. The spirit's words are reproduced with distinctive prosodic features: there is increased volume, indicating excitement and the sense that making contact is important to the spirit; the significance of the communication is certainly affirmed by the words of the spirit. Furthermore, the medium's comments on the prosodic features of the reported speech [suggest] . . . personality embodied or reflected in the words themselves and the way they were said. . . .

Silence Is Risky for Mediums

Finally, I want to make some brief remarks about how reported speech may be used to manage interactional episodes which could at the very least be interpreted as evidence disconfirming the medium's paranormal powers.

Jefferson (1989) has observed that participants in ordinary interaction may treat absences of talk which extend to approximately one second as indicating some form of difficulty or trouble in the exchange. This 'metric' may also be observed during medium-sitter interaction. In the following extract the medium's proposal about the spirit of the sitter's aunt does not receive either an acceptance or a rejection but silence. After 1.2 seconds (the upper limit of Jefferson's tolerance interval) the medium produces a revised proposal: 'I feel that when she went, she was just tired.'

There are risks in this strategy: if a medium makes a substantive claim which does not accord with the sitter's knowledge or experience, there is at least a basis for questioning the extent and genuineness of his or her powers. Moreover, if, having monitored the sitter's silence, the medium then proposes an alternative or revised knowledge claim, they may be open to the charge that they are guessing, or merely amending their utterances in light of what can be plainly inferred from the sitter's silence. Thus, the acceptance of any subsequent knowledge claim is an inferentially sensitive moment; and it is here that the spirit's words may be incorporated to endorse explicitly the revised claim.

[Extract 9]

> M: and your aunt was was such a sick lady before she passed.
> [1.2 seconds pass]
>
> M: I feel that when she went . . . [1.5 seconds pass]

M: she was just tired.

S: yes

M: that's what she tells me. She said "I was so

S: [Yes]

M: tired. [.6 seconds pass]

M: I didn't [want to] eat[;] I didn't want to do anything. [.3 seconds pass]

M: I just was tired.

S: mm hm

M: I'd had enough. [S]o I think [I'd]—whatever they put on her death certificate it would've [.3 seconds pass]

M: Really the answer was she gave up she didn't want

S: [Yes]

M: to live any more. She'd had enough

S: [had enough] had enough

M: hhh ((*clears throat*)) I think she might have had a little stroke, because I can feel as if something went

S: yes: she did [.3 seconds pass]

M: but again it was just something to herald the end and ellen.

Both of the medium's proposals deal with ostensibly the same topic: the condition of the sitter's aunt prior to her death. However, there is a significant amendment, in that the first implies that ill health was the cause of death, and as such makes a specific claim. The second proposes only that the aunt's demise was associated with tiredness, which implies the death was due to natural [aging]. The medium has interpreted the silence following the first proposal as displaying the sitter's inability or reluctance to accept it; the second proposal offers an alternative and less specific account of the spirit's death. It is also prefaced by 'I feel' which modulates the epistemological status of the proposal, and is again in contrast to the more declarative design of the first proposal. The sitter accepts the second proposal. Then, in the third position turn, the medium states that the spirit is saying that she was tired, and then introduces the spirit's voice as confirmation. . . .

Conclusion: Mediums Use Verbal Strategies

Providing evidence of the sentient dead to the living is the *sine qua non* [or indispensable action] of mediumship; reproducing their words is one of the practices by which this can be achieved. Given its central importance to the work of the medium, it is no surprise, then, that a key method by which this institutional requirement is met exhibits robust organizational properties. Moreover, the voices of the dead are used to address a limited range of inferential tasks broadly concerned with establishing the authority and authenticity of the medium.

In this analysis I have not attempted to debunk the mediums' claims, (although the analytic focus on the social organization of their discourse invariably lends itself to appropriation by a sceptical audience) but to describe one property of the way in which they are managed. This agnostic position has been adopted in order to expose for analysis those discursive practices which sustain the lived experience of mediumship, and, thereby, to generate a new range of topics for empirical enquiry by which we can come to a more sophisticated appreciation not only of mediumship, but of the work of psychic practitioners more generally. To conclude, then, I want to make some more general remarks concerning the analytic perspective adopted in this article, and to sketch some further lines of inquiry.

Heritage (1997) has identified three criteria by which it is possible to demarcate ordinary conversational interaction from talk which occurs in institutional or work-related settings. A consideration of these criteria, and their relevance to medium-sitter interaction, allows us to identify a range of empirically investigable issues. First, participants in institutional interaction are normally concerned with a specific set of tasks and goals which are clearly connected to the 'business' of the institution; moreover, these goals are tied to identities relevant to that institution. While mediums are not necessarily perceived as working in formal institutions such as hospitals or courtrooms, we may begin to investigate how their discourse is concerned with a fairly well-defined set of goals; moreover, we can begin to explore the ways in which the verbal activities of a sitting mobilize the relevance of a strictly observed set of identities. Second, Heritage notes that in institutional talk it is understood that there are constraints on what kinds of participation are normatively appropriate. Again, there are parallels with medium-sitter interaction, in which, for example, it is understood that only one party will be expected to provide information derived from a paranormal source. But we can ask: what other normative requirements are addressed and met by the design of participants' contributions? Finally, the participants' conduct in a sitting is informed by the expectation that it is a vehicle for confirmation of the spirit afterlife: and this reflects Heritage's observation that the practical tasks or business of the institution will shape the kinds of inferences about and understanding of ongoing interaction. Medium-sitter interaction, then, may be characterized as a form of institutional discourse, albeit of a non-formal kind (Drew and Heritage, 1992: 27). Consequently, in the same way that institutional talk can be investigated to explore how its organization manages the business of the institution, and thereby mobilizes the concerns of the institution as interactionally relevant matters for participants, so too can these features of medium-sitter interaction be analysed to reveal the socially organized practices which sustain the (quasi-institutional) demonstration of the sentient and co-present spirit world. The analysis of the reproduction of the spirits' words in mediums' discourse has been a first step in that task.

Notes

1. The idea that some special people can communicate with the dead is a common motif throughout history. However, the characteristics and practices of what is now recognized as mediumship date back to the 1840s when two young sisters from Hydesville in New York State became the apparent focus for a series of strange rappings and knockings. The sisters seemed to be able to communicate with the source of the noises, which revealed itself to be a spirit. The sisters quickly became celebrities and demonstrations of their skills were in great demand. When they visited other cities the noises appeared to follow them, and they were able to engage in conversations with the dead through the knocks and raps produced by their spirits. In the wake of their popularity and their travels, many other individuals claimed to communicate with the spirits of the dead and this ability came to be known as mediumship. The popularity and fame of spiritualism grew, spreading across the United States and eventually to Europe, popularizing the possibility that people could, in some form, survive death.
2. The data in this article come from a wider study of the discourse of psychic practitioners. All data extracts come from recordings of private sittings between mediums and one (or two) clients. Extracts identified by the DS/AUD prefix come from public demonstrations of mediumship in theatres. (For an account of the various data sources, see Wooffitt, 2000.)
3. Indeed, sitters adopt a conspicuously passive stance given the apparent co-presence of the spirit of a relative or spouse. This should not be taken to imply, however, that the sitters are displaying scepticism in withholding participation in the sitting: in the present corpus there are instances of sitters adopting a passive role during the sitting but later articulating their belief that they had witnessed a convincing demonstration that the spirit of a loved one was communicating with them through the medium.

References

1. J.E. Best, *Link and Communiqué: A Personal Psychic Experience*. London: Regency, 1991.
2. R. Buttny, "Putting Prior Talk into Context: Reported Speech and Reporting Context," *Research on Language and Social Interaction*, vol. 31, no. 1, 1998.
3. R. Buttny and P.L. Williams, "Demanding Respect: The Uses of Reported Speech in Discursive Constructions of Interracial Contact," *Discourse & Society*, vol. 11, no. 1, 2000.
4. M. Christopher, *ESP, Seers, and Psychics: What the Occult Really Is*. New York: Thomas Y. Crowell, 1970.

5. M. Christopher, *Mediums, Mystics, and the Occult*. New York: Thomas Y. Crowell, 1975.

6. S.E. Clayman, "Footing in the Achievement of Neutrality: The Case of News Interview Discourse," in P. Drew and J. Heritage, eds., *Talk at Work: Interaction in Institutional Settings*. Cambridge, UK: Cambridge University Press, 1992.

7. F. Coulmas, "Reported Speech: Some General Issues," in F. Coulmas, ed., *Direct and Indirect Speech*. Berlin: Mouton de Gruyter, 1986.

8. P. Drew and J. Heritage, *Talk at Work: Interaction in Institutional Settings*. Cambridge, UK: Cambridge University Press, 1992.

9. S. Ellison, *The Reality of the Paranormal*. London: Harrap, 1988.

10. E. Goffman, "Footing," in E. Goffman, ed., *Forms of Talk*. Oxford, UK: Blackwell, 1981.

11. J. Heritage, "Conversation Analysis and Institutional Talk: Analysing Data," in D. Silverman, ed., *Qualitative Research: Theory, Method, and Practice*. London: Sage, 1997.

12. J. Heritage and D. Greatbatch, "On the Institutional Character of Institutional Talk: The Case of News Interviews," in D. Boden and D. Zimmerman, eds., *Talk and Social Structure*. Cambridge, UK: Polity, 1991.

13. E. Holt, "Reporting on Talk: The Use of Direct Reported Speech in Conversation," *Research on Language and Social Interaction*, vol. 29, no. 3, 1996.

14. R. Hyman, "'Cold Reading': How to Convince Strangers That You Know All About Them," in K. Frazier, ed., *Paranormal Borderlands of Science*. New York: Prometheus, 1981.

15. G. Jefferson, "Notes on a Possible Metric for a Standard Maximum Silence of Approximately One Second in Conversation," in D. Roger and P. Bull, eds., *Conversation: an Interdisciplinary Perspective*. Clevedon, UK: Multilingual Matters, 1989.

16. M. Keen, A. Ellison, and D. Fontana, "The Scole Report," *Proceedings of the Society for Psychical Research*, vol. 58, no. 220, 1999.

17. A. Lehrer, "Remembering and Representing Prose: Quoted Speech as a Data Source," *Discourse Processes*, vol. 12, 1989.

18. I. Leudar, "Who Is Martin McGuiness? On Contextualizing Reported Political Talk," in S. Cmejrkova et al., ed., *Dialogue Analysis 6*, vol. 2. Tubingen, Germany: Niemeyer, 1998.

19. C.N. Li, "Direct and Indirect Speech: A Functional Study," in F. Coulmas, ed., *Direct and Indirect Speech*. Berlin: Mouton de Gruyter, 1986.

20. P. Mayes, "Quotation in Spoken English," *Studies in Language*, vol. 14, no. 2, 1990.

21. G. Myers, "Functions of Reported Speech in Group Discussions," *Applied Linguistics*, vol. 20, no. 3, 1999.

22. S. O'Brien, *In Touch with Eternity: Contact with Another World*. London: Bantam, 1992.

23. S.U. Phillips, "Reported Speech as Evidence in an American Trial." In D. Tannen and J.E. Alatis, eds., *Languages and Linguistics: The Interdependence of Theory, Data, and Application*. Washington, DC: Georgetown University Press, 1986.

24. J. Potter, *Representing Reality: Discourse, Rhetoric, and Social Construction*. London: Sage, 1996.

25. J. Randi, "Cold Reading Revisited," in K. Frazier, ed., *Paranormal Borderlands of Science*. New York: Prometheus, 1981.

26. C.A. Roe, "Pseudopsychics and the Barnum Effect," *European Journal of Para-psychology*, vol. 11, 1995.

27. E.A. Schegloff, "Goffman and the Analysis of Conversation," in P. Drew and T., Wootton, eds., *Erving Goffman: Exploring the Interaction Order*. Cambridge, UK: Polity, 1988.

28. D. Tannen, "Introducing Constructed Dialogue in Greek and American Conversational and Literary Narrative," in F. Coulmas, ed., *Direct and Indirect Speech*. Berlin: Mouton de Gruyter, 1986.

29. R. Wooffitt, *Telling Tales of the Unexpected: The Organisation of Factual Discourse*. Hemel Hempstead, UK: Harvester Wheatsheaf, 1992.

30. R. Wooffitt, "A Socially Organised Basis for Displays of Cognition: Procedural Orientation to Evidential Turns in Psychic-Sitter Interaction." *British Journal of Social Psychology*, 2001.

Epilogue: Analyzing the Evidence

Many people say that communication with the spirit world is a hoax, and a long list of mediums have had their credibility shattered by skeptics who figured out their tricks. In the nineteenth century, scientist Michael Faraday proved that mediums and table tipping were a hoax. At the time, mediums claimed that in a séance, a spirit would move a table to prove its presence. Faraday had other ideas:

> He theorized that the motive force for table turning was the involuntary and unconscious muscle contractions of séance sitters who wanted the table to move. To demonstrate, he fashioned a table with two tops that were divided by a layer of ball bearings and joined by stout rubber bands. When séance sitters worked with the device, the upper tabletop moved first, showing that fingers were moving the table and not vice versa. Moroeover, once the sitters knew the nature of the experiment, movement ceased.[1] Soon, other phenomena were also debunked: In the Victorian era, mediums worked almost exclusively in dark rooms or in "medium's cabinets" that hid them from full view. Using a foot to lift a table or using an extending rod to make an object "float" were standard tricks that could not be replicated with lights on or cabinet doors open. Scientific skeptics were learning that one way to investigate mediums was to change one element of the atmosphere (lighting, for example) and see if the mediums could replicate the phenomena. Some could, but most could not.

Experiments like Faraday's seem airtight. He used physics, logic, and simple observation—all the hallmarks of rational problem-solving. However, there is one big problem that both skeptics and believers face, regardless of controlled experiments: the *confirmation bias.*

What Is Confirmation Bias?

To begin to answer that question, consider the following event. The year was 1960. The spiritualist town of Camp Chesterfield, Indiana, was a hot-spot for mediums who lived and worked there exclusively. That July, thousands of paying tourists visited for readings and encounters with the spirit world, but some unwitting supporters were about to expose fraud. Ironically, it wouldn't matter. Former medium M. Lamar Keene recounted the situation:

> Two sympathetic researchers, Tom O'Neill and Dr. Andrija Puharich, had tried to get the first motion pictures ever of the materialization of a spirit. [They] went into a dark séance room equipped with infrared lights and film [. . .] Peering through the snooperscope in the dark, Puharich saw that what were supposed to be spirit forms of shimmering ectoplasm materializing out of thin air, were actually figures wrapped in chiffon entering the séance room through a hidden door [. . .] Tom O'Neill, the devout spiritualist, was devastated by the revelations. He who had believed implicitly in the phenomena now raged against the "frauds, fakes, and fantasies [. . .]."[2] With Chesterfield on the verge of closing, M. Lamar Keene and his business partner stepped in to save the camp. "We used all kinds of explanations to conjure away the damning film footage," explains Keene in *The Psychic Mafia*, his tell-all memoir of life as a fraudulent medium. Keene claimed that it was trick photography, and that O'Neill was under pressure from the Catholic Church, among other explanations. He didn't back up his claims. No matter—the staff and patrons rallied behind Keene, and Chesterfield weathered the controversy as if it never happened. "The exposé rather than ruining business, actually improved it," remembers Keene.[3]

What allows people to come to a conclusion contrary to evidence? It's the confirmation bias—you seek out facts, opinions, and information that support what you want to believe, and you discredit or disregard contradictory statements. Another version of the confirmation bias is that you champion an occurrence while downplaying a nonoccurrence, or vice versa, if it helps your case. Michael Shermer, a skeptic and author of the book *Why Smart People Believe Weird Things*, explains that facts come "through the colored filters of the theories, hypotheses, hunches, biases, and prejudices we have accumulated through our lifetime. We then sort through the body of data and select those most confirming what we already believe, and ignore or rationalize away those that are disconfirming."[4]

So powerful is the need to believe what we already believe that everyone from superstitious alarmists to scholarly researchers can be swayed by the confirmation bias. For example, you may have noted that skeptics in this book got very specific with their criticisms. Robin Wooffitt, for example, used myopically precise language analysis to only *begin* to make a case against a few mediums. Wooffitt studies language for a living, so he might be biased toward making much of any conclusion, no matter how minor, because that is what he was trained to do in the first place. His entire career has been built around explaining patterns in language, so might it say more about him (and not so much about mediums) that he's detected patterns in their speaking?

Getting Past Confirmation Bias

It's not as hard as you might think. The trick is to be honest with yourself about your biases and remember them when you have a reaction to a viewpoint in this book. Were you raised in a family that valued practical, rational thinking over emotional reactions? If so, you might at first doubt the emotional support behind mediums. Think carefully, however—is the doubt coming from evidence in the viewpoint, or is it coming from your own background? If you can honestly say that your doubt is coming from evidence given by the author, then you don't have a confirmation bias.

Another way to overcome confirmation bias is to practice a technique called reading against the grain. Think of a piece of wood. It has a texture, or grain, that is smooth if you rub it one direction and rough the other. You might get splinters if you rub against the grain. When you read with the grain, you follow the smooth path the author intended you to follow, in agreement with the author. When reading against the grain, think of ways to debate what the author is saying. Raise contentions, ask questions. Get a few splinters, and learn lessons from them. You might not actually disagree, but that's the point. Read as if you disagree. Role-play the pros and cons of an argument.

Learn to recognize the confirmation bias in other people. Here is a good question to ask as you read a viewpoint: If this author had to retract the entire argument, what would be at stake? Would the author lose her job? Would he be cast out of a community or professional society? Would there be a financial loss? The more there is at stake, the stronger a confirmation bias could be. Take, for example, historian David Fontana, whose viewpoint supports mediums. Fontana is an author of a few books about supernatural happenings. He's been active in the Society for Psychical Research (SPR). He's a professor. If he suddenly retracted his opinion about mediums, he would have many critics to answer to—his book editor, his colleagues in the SPR, his students, and his own conscience. Joe Nickell, whose viewpoint is against mediums, works for the magazine *Skeptical Inquirer*. If he changed his mind, he would have to find another magazine to write for.

Anecdotal Evidence

When you tell an anecdote, you are telling a brief, true story of events. Many of the viewpoints, pro and con, contain anecdotes. Why is that? The author is hoping you will connect on a personal, private level, as if a trusted friend is telling you this information. Anecdotes can be powerful—simple story-telling is the foundation of how we learn about each other. As evidence, it cannot be dismissed, but how seriously can it be taken? People perceive anecdotes as first-hand evidence, and sometimes that's more influential than any Nobel Prize winner's research.

When you encounter anecdotal evidence, think about word choice, use of emotions, and use of dialogue. Combined, these things make up the tone of the piece. Studying the tone is a good way to analyze anecdotes. Consider this sentence written by a skeptic who visited a medium in order to write a humorous commentary about the experience: "A palpable embarrassment fills the air, as if we are sitting in the waiting room of a sexually transmitted diseases clinic."[5] Note the dark humor when he compares waiting for the medium to waiting for bad (and embarrassing) health news. Do you think the writer is taking this visit seriously? Can you trust his reaction to the medium?

If you decide to read more accounts written by mediums, you might notice a trend—mediums often reference scenes from popular movies, and they drop names of celebrities. Bank on a medium claiming to have contacted Princess Diana, or some other tragically deceased public figure. You could conclude that the medium heard from Princess Diana. But is there another motive? There might be. Think of Princess Diana's worldwide popularity, the ubiquity of her photo. Remember her shocking death at a young age, how it made headline news around the world. Who does her story appeal to? Could her story appeal to the same audience that is interested in mediums? If a medium wants to reach a wide audience, he or she needs to appeal to a wide audience. When mediums make glittery claims of contacting dead celebrities, be twice as wary. They could be using star-appeal to get more people to buy their books or attend their seminars.

Another good point to study when it comes to anecdotal evidence is something called locus of control. Skeptic Michael Shermer says that, "People who measure high on the external locus of control tend to believe that circumstances are beyond their control and that things just happen to them. People who measure high on the internal locus of control tend to believe they are in control of their circumstances and that they make things happen."[6] If you lean toward the external locus of control, you would be more willing to believe in mediums. Can you reason why? If you go to a medium to get a message, you are acknowledging that you cannot receive the message yourself—you have to rely on an external source. Shermer notes that, "A 1983 study by Jerome Tobacyk and Gary Milford of introductory psychology students at Louisiana Tech University, for example, found that those who scored high in external locus of control tended to believe in ESP, witchcraft, spiritualism, reincarnation, precognition, and were more superstitious than those students who scored high in internal locus of control."[7]

Finally, notice that in anecdotes, people refer to "having a feeling" or "just knowing in my heart" that such-and-such was accurate. Call it intuition, premonition, or a gut reaction—we've all experienced it. How much weight should you give such a feeling? French critics and skeptics Georges Charpak and Henri Broch caution that "reasoning by sensation" is dangerous. When you reason by sensation, a visual stimulus creates a physical sensation, and then you make decisions based on the physical sensation. "But just because you act on 'gut feelings' is no reason to keep you from also working with your brain."[8]

Scientific Evidence

When mediums first announced their abilities in the nineteenth century, members of the scientific community wasted no time requesting experiments and coming to conclusions.

Ever since the Age of Enlightenment, scientific proof (or disproof) has been held in high regard. Most people trust the scientific method, and they trust that repeated experiments that use controls will produce accurate results. On the other hand, some supporters contend that the scientific method has limitations and is not suitable for supernatural phenomena. Could they be right? Other supporters have conducted rigorous experiments where mediums have had success rates that exceed lucky guessing. Maybe they are right. But then there is a skeptic, James Randi, who has a million dollar prize available right now for the first medium who can indisputably prove, to Randi's satisfaction, that communication with the spirit world is possible. Randi, a magician, has found fraud in every attempt for his prize.

Recently, however, some very credible and educated researchers have made rigorous attempts to test mediums. They have respectable credentials, such as advanced college degrees and careers at universities—accomplishments that took time, effort, and dedication. But should you always assume that a smart person has come to a smart conclusion?

Skeptic Michael Shermer says no. "Smart people believe weird things because they are skilled at defending beliefs they arrive at for non-smart reasons. . . . Another problem is that smart people might be smart in only one field. We say that their intelligence is domain specific."[9] So, when analyzing evidence, do seek out viewpoints by educated, credible people; pay attention, however, to how they make their cases and to their areas of expertise.

Testing mediums presents unique difficulties. First, just trying to observe, measure, and quantify exactly what mediums are doing is a huge challenge. To put it in perspective, imagine conducting a simple experiment with two plants— one will get water, and the other won't. Every day, you can measure the height, count leaves, and describe whether the plant is wilted or not. Basically, you have confidence that you can trust what you are observing.

But how do you apply the scientific method to mediums? Mediums tell us that communications from the spirit world are telepathic—no verbal sounds, but rather a mental awareness of a message or image. That means the messages cannot be observed or evaluated by a non-medium. Mediums also say that success is partly due to spirits being willing to participate. Again, how would researchers evaluate this variable? The researcher, not being a medium, has no awareness of the spirits. It's a difficult situation; a good science experiment with mediums would actually require the tester to have some mediumistic abilities, which would negate the need for the experiment in the first place.

Another conundrum when it comes to scientific evidence and mediums is the single-blind, double-blind requirement. To explain these concepts, let's use a medical experiment as our example: say you have a weight-loss pill you need to test. In a single-blind experiment, some of your subjects would take the weight-loss pill, and some would take a placebo (a fake pill that won't make any changes), but no one would know which pill they were getting. They are blind to which pill is which. In a double-blind experiment, not even you know who is getting which pill. An assistant distributes the pills, and you receive the data. Only after you analyze the data would you let yourself learn who took which pill.

Single-blind experiments eliminate participant bias; double-blind experiments eliminate participant bias *and* researcher bias. When you read a scientific claim about mediums, pay attention to how the experiment was conducted. Few involve any levels of blind, because that's difficult to do with humans and spirits. However, if it were single-blind, chances of fraud have been decreased; double-blind cuts further opportunities to cheat; and if there weren't any levels of blind involved, be cautious of the conclusions.

Religious Evidence

Religion teaches us that our actions now will determine our location later. If you believe in an afterlife, you would certainly wonder how your loved ones are fairing up there (or down there). People go to mediums in a search for knowledge that the afterlife exists, as centuries of religious teachings have suggested, and that it's a pleasant existence where good deeds on earth are rewarded, in one form or another, with a celestial paradise.

But what do theologians say about mediums? Rabbi Marc Gellman had answers on two sides of the question. In support of mediums, Gellman recounted the biblical story of King Saul seeking help from the dead prophet Samuel. Saul wanted guidance for an upcoming battle, so he consulted a witch, who invoked Samuel's spirit to appear. "Saul's plea to the ghost of Samuel, 'I have called on you to tell me what I should do,' is a plea I have heard from other people to other ghosts at other times of terror," concluded Gellman.[10] We want to seek advice from the deceased because we assume that they have overarching wisdom about mortal affairs. Saul's story is not so different from praying to a deceased loved one for advice.

But on the other hand, Gellman believes that we need to take death seriously, and mediums don't show the proper respect. "Death is an existential, spiritual, ontological boundary line we are not intended to or permitted to cross while we are alive; talking to dead people makes a spiritual mockery of that boundary. For this reason the Bible that speaks of ghosts also speaks of how we should not try to contact them or deal with people who think they have an open line to them that we can . . . rent."[11]

Read carefully, however. This example doesn't argue against mediums existing—it argues against *dealing* with mediums. It is counseling us to use good judgment and to respect death. Whether or not mediums respect death is beside the point when it comes to proving or disproving their abilities. As skeptic James Randi explained, it "is much like measuring chimneys to determine whether a fat man in a red suit can get down them, and to thereby explore the reality of Santa Claus."[12] Just because a chimney *could* be wide enough for Santa doesn't mean that Santa is real. Just because mediums violate the Old Testament's guidelines for respect doesn't mean that they are frauds.

As you read skeptics' claims against mediums, pay careful attention to tangential arguments masquerading as main arguments. The skeptic might be committing a logical fallacy known as a red herring. When an argument is misleading, it is a red herring. For example, it is easy to get caught up in the debate about how to respect death. You can probably think of many examples of respect and disrespect, and you might have a strong, well-supported opinion. But, in the end, whether mediums respect or disrespect the dead has little to do with their actual ability to contact the dead.

Mediums and Cheating

There's no way around it: mediums have been caught cheating. Not all of them, not all the time, but their credibility has been damaged. As a result, experiments with mediums have to focus on eliminating fraud as much as they focus on testing mediums' abilities. Do you think that all the emphasis on fraud has been unfair to mediums? Can a researcher accurately observe what's happening when he or she is distracted by having to double-check safeguards meant to prevent trickery?

One medium from the nineteenth century was brazen in her cheating, but, when she wished, she wowed observers with what appeared to be authentic phenomena. Her name was Eusapia Palladino, and her abilities confounded the brightest researchers of the time. "Eusapia cheated, she cheated often, she even admitted cheating. But after her fraudulent phenomena were explained away, a residue remained, inexplicable happenings that raised the nagging question: *Did she cheat all the time?*"[13] Palladino's talent was invoking spirits to make objects move. Her researchers observed many instances when, with Palladino's hands and feet bound and lights on, objects still moved around the room. No one could explain it. Like the case of the Camp Chesterfield fraud, Palladino had loyal supporters who refused to condemn her for cheating. "Of course she cheated, they argued. When her powers were low, she often cheated as an easier alternative to expending the energy required for genuine phenomena. Investigators had already discovered this weakness. . . . Did they not see that the very clumsiness of her cheating belied her being an accomplished fraud?"[14]

So, when analyzing evidence, you might find instances where you can make the case for cheating, or at least the opportunity to cheat. However, if another piece of evidence appears authentic, what do you conclude? To say that all mediums cheat because one medium cheated is a logical fallacy known as a generalization, and it is just what it sounds like—a hasty jump to a general conclusion that applies to some, but not all. Skeptical arguments against mediums are frequently based on hasty generalizations, so learn to recognize them. Supporters make the mistake too. Receiving one encouraging reading and then assuming that all mediums are authentic would be a hasty generalization. Remember the earlier discussion on how to analyze anecdotal evidence? Anecdotes and hasty generalizations go together like two pieces of a puzzle. One can tip you off to the other.

The debate about mediums is not an easy one to resolve. Sifting through the evidence requires strong critical thinking skills. Because the abilities of mediums are so difficult to test in a scientific setting, much of your evidence will come from subjective accounts, not objective test results. Any time that the subjective takes the field, you have to contend with emotions, opinions, faulty assumptions, and powerful belief systems. All that can be intimidating, but also energizing and fascinating. Think of mediums as a great mystery to be explored, and explore them well.

Notes

1. *Mysteries of the Unknown: Spirit Summoning*. Alexandria, VA: Time-Life Books, 1989, p. 33.
2. M. Lamar Keene, *The Psychic Mafia*. Amherst, NY: Prometheus Books, 1997, p. 40.
3. M. Lamar Keene, *The Psychic Mafia*. p. 42.
4. Michael Shermer, "Why Smart People Believe Weird Things," *Skeptic*, Summer 2003; accessed via *InfoTrac OneFile*, November 21, 2005.
5. Peter Stanford, "Knock, Knock, Who's There? A Dead Man's Spirit," *New Stateman*, April 2002, p. 32.
6. Michael Shermer, "Why Smart People Believe Weird Things."
7. Michael Shermer, "Why Smart People Believe Weird Things."
8. Georges Charpak and Henri Broch, *Debunked! ESP, Telekinesis, and Other Pseudoscience*, trans. Bart K. Holland, Baltimore: John Hopkins University Press, 2004, p. 121.
9. Michael Shermer, "Why Smart People Believe Weird Things."
10. Marc Gellman, "Dialing for Dead People," *Newsweek*, Feb. 9, 2005; Society section of the Web site; accessed via *Lexis-Nexis*, December 19, 2005.
11. Marc Gellman, "Dialing for Dead People."
12. James Randi, "May the Schwartz Be with You," *Skeptic*, vol. 9, 2001; accessed via *EBSCOhost*, May 26, 2006.
13. *Mysteries of the Unknown: Spirit Summonings*, p. 58.
14. *Mysteries of the Unknown: Spirit Summonings*, pp. 62-63.

Glossary

Akashic Records The supposed cosmic memory storage area of all the thoughts and actions of everyone who has ever lived.

apports Objects from the spirit world, usually materialized by a medium and often of relevance to the sitter.

automatic writing Writing produced by a medium in a trance, the message of which supposedly comes from a spirit.

channeler A person who lets a discarnate personality communicate through them; as distinct from a medium, a channeler assumes the voice and sometimes the language of the spirit.

cold reading Making assumptions based on a sitter's appearance, body language, or vocabulary, and rephrasing those assumptions as communication from a spirit; a method of fraud.

discarnate Not having a flesh-and-blood body.

ectoplasm A substance thought to materialize from a medium when communicating with the dead.

hit When a medium makes an accurate statement.

hot reading A method of fraud where a medium researches a sitter prior to a reading, memorizing information, then pretending the information is coming from a spirit.

medium A person who claims to be able to communicate with the spirit world.

medium's cabinet Invented by escape-artist brothers William and Ira Davenport, a medium's cabinet held one or two people bound and locked inside. Noises and mysterious illusions then came from the cabinet. Mediums claimed that the cabinet was essential for capturing psychic energy.

mediumistic espionage Term coined by former medium M. Lamar Keene, this is a type of fraud. It happens when mediums spy on clients to get personal information or when mediums exchange information on clients.

mental mediums Mediums who receive verbal messages from the spirit world.

New Age A wide-ranging movement from the 1980s that includes channelers, mediums, crystals, talismans, and other accoutrements of a newfound spiritual connection.

physical mediums Mediums who verify that they are in contact with spirits by displaying visual phenomena. They can move and manipulate objects (ectoplasm, light, furniture) without touching the objects. They can also produce apports, or objects that seem to come out of nowhere.

sitter A person who receives a reading from a medium.

sleight of mind A term developed by skeptics to explain, by analogy to a magician's sleight of hand, what it is that mediums are really doing.

spirit The personality that remains after the death of the physical body.

spirit revelation The information the medium receives from a spirit.

spirit writing *see* automatic writing.

spiritism A religious offshoot of spiritualism that believes that mediums are an active part of religious worship and moral education; they are against mediums charging for services.

Spiritualism A movement that believes the human spirit survives death and can communicate with the living.

trance writing *see* automatic writing.

For Further Reading

Books

Diane Arcangel, *After Life Encounters: Ordinary People, Extraordinary Encounters*. Charlottesville, VA: Hampton Roads, 2005.

George E. Dalzell and Gary Schwartz, *Messages: Evidence for Life After Death*. Charlottesville, VA: Hampton Roads, 2002.

Allison DuBois, *Don't Kiss Them Good-bye*. New York: Fireside, 2005.

Allison DuBois, *We Are Their Heaven: Why the Dead Never Leave Us*. New York: Fireside, 2006.

John Edward, *Crossing Over: The Stories Behind the Stories*. Carlsbad, CA: Hay House, 2003.

Agnes Freeman, *The Fledgling's Way to Mediumship: How to Become a Good and Honest Psychic Medium*. Market Harborough, UK: Matador, 2003.

Terrence Hines, *Pseudoscience and the Paranormal*. Amherst, NY: Prometheus Books, 2003.

John Holland and Cindy Pearlman, *A Medium's Journey: Accepting and Embracing My Spiritual Gifts*. Carlsbad, CA: Hay House, 2003.

Terry Iacuzzo, *Small Mediums at Large: The True Tales of a Family of Psychics*. New York: Putnam Adult, 2004.

Peter Lamont, *The First Psychic: The Peculiar Mystery of a Notorious Victorian Wizard*. London: Little, Brown, 2005.

Carole Lynne, *How to Get a Good Reading from a Psychic Medium: Get the Most Out of Your Contact with the Other Side*. Boston: Weiser, 2003.

MaryRose Occhino, *Beyond These Four Walls: Diary of a Psychic Medium.* New York: Berkley, 2004

Edward Olshaker, *Witness to the Unsolved: Prominent Psychic Detectives and Mediums Explore Our Most Haunting Mysteries.* Owings Mills, MD: Remiel, 2005.

Moriah Rhame-Brock, *How to Be a Happy Medium.* Chicago: Pendragon, 2004.

Ron Rhodes, *The Truth Behind Ghosts, Mediums, and Psychic Phenomena.* Eugene, OR: Harvest House, 2006.

Theodore Schick, *How to Think About Weird Things.* New York: McGraw-Hill Humanities, 2002.

Michael Shermer, ed., *The Skeptic Encyclopedia of Pseudoscience.* Santa Barbara, CA: ABC-CLIO, 2004.

Gordon Smith, *Spirit Messenger.* Carlsbad, CA: Hay House, 2004.

Tony Stockwell, *Spirited: Living Between Two Worlds; a Top Psychic Medium's Extraordinary Story.* London: Hodder Mobius, 2005.

Victoria Lynn Weston, *Akashic Who's Who of Psychics, Mediums, Healers, and More!* New York: iUniverse, 2005.

Christine Wicker, *Lily Dale: The True Story of the Town That Talks to the Dead.* New York: HarperCollins, 2003.

Periodicals

Heather R. Auton, Jacqueline Pope, and Gus Seeger, "It Isn't That Strange: Paranormal Belief and Personality Traits," *Social Behavior & Personality: An International Journal,* 2003.

Carole Braden, "Real-life 'Mediums,'" *Good Housekeeping,* November 2005.

Paola Bressan, "The Connections Between Random Sequences, Everyday Coincidences, and Belief in the Paranormal," *Applied Cognitive Psychology*, January 2002.

Bill Briggs, "Solving Crimes: Tall Tales of True Medium? Self-Proclaimed Psychic Says She Can 'See' Killers," *Denver Post*, August 1, 2002.

Mike Chappel, "Row over TV Psychic's Bid to Contact Lennon Spirit," *Daily Post* (Liverpool, UK), April 17, 2006.

"CSICOP Timeline: A Capsule History in 85 Easy Steps," *Skeptical Inquirer*, May/June 2001.

Samantha Dunn, "The Medium Has a Message," *O: The Oprah Magazine*, May 2006.

Kendrick Frazier, "Death of the Afterlife Experiments?" *Skeptical Inquirer*, January/February 2003.

Bill Gilbert, "In Good Spirits," *Smithsonian*, June 2001.

Angus Haddow, "Should Christianity Embrace Mediumship, Healing, and Reincarnation?" *Proceedings (Academy of Spirituality & Paranormal Studies)*, 2004.

William Harwood, "A Closer Look at Mediums," *Skeptical Inquirer*, May/June 2005.

Mark Henderson, "Scientific Tests Cloud Mediums' Crystal Balls," *Ottawa (ON) Citizen*, September 23, 2004.

Ray Hyman, "How Not to Test Mediums: Critiquing the Afterlife Experiments," *Skeptical Inquirer*, January/February 2003.

Montague Keen, "The Academy of Psychic and Religious Sources on Life After Death," *Proceedings (Academy of Spirituality & Paranormal Studies)*, 2003.

Elizabeth Kuster and Anuradha Koli, "Psychic Ability: So Some People Really Have It?" *Cosmopolitan*, June 2005.

Reed Lucy, *"Spirits Help City Man Speak for the Dead,"* *Waikato Times* (New Zealand), June 25, 2005.

Hilary Mantel, "Unearthly Powers," *New Statesman*, August 29, 2005.

Barry Markovsky and Shane R. Thye, "Social Influence on Paranormal Beliefs," *Sociological Perspectives*, Spring 2001.

Robert W. Newby and Jessica Boyette Davis, "Relationships Between Locus of Control and Paranormal Beliefs," *Psychological Reports*, June 2004.

Lee Nisbet, "The Origins and Evolution of CSICOP," *Skeptical Inquirer*, November/December 2001.

Kenneth Oldfield, "Philosophers and Psychics: The Vandy Episode," *Skeptical Inquirer*, November/December 2001.

Tania Padgett, "The Mediums Are Getting the Message," *Newsday*, June 7, 2006

Linda Peterson, "A Conversation with Psychic Medium John Edward," *Biography*, April 2002.

Brady J. Phelps, Elizabeth C. Wogen, and Scott C. Pedersen, "Dead Silence: Our Experience at a 'Live' Seminar with John Edward," *Skeptic*, Summer 2003.

Enola Pirog, *"Should You Consult Psychics? Mediums?"* *Journal of Religion & Psychical Research*, April 2004.

James Poniewozik, "Spirits of the Age," *Time*, February 14, 2005.

Proceedings (Academy of Spirituality & Paranormal Studies), "Panel Mediumship: A Window to Other Dimensions of Existence," 2004.

Ruth Reinsel, "Mediumistic Phenomena Circa 2002," *Proceedings (The Academy of Religion & Psychical Research)*, 2004.

Gary E.R. Schwartz, Linda G. S. Russek, "Celebrating Susy Smith's Soul: Preliminary Evidence for the Continuation of Smith's Consciousness After Her Physical Death," *Journal of Religion & Psychical Research*, April 2001.

Stephen Schwartz, "Spirit World," *American Heritage*. April/May 2005.

Skeptical Inquirer, "The Ten Outstanding Skeptics of the Twentieth Century," January/February 2000.

Alessandra Stanley, "Using Death to Connect the Living," *New York Times*, April 5, 2006.

Index

afterlife
  evidence of communication
    with, problem of, 12–13
  religion as basis for belief in,
    10, 12
Afterlife Experiments, The, 29
Afterlife Experiments, The
  (Schwartz), 56, 87
Akhtar, M., 42
Althea, Rosemary, 88
ancestor worship, 50–51
Anderson, George, 60, 68, 91
apparitions, 78

Ballard, Chris, 105
Barentsen, Christopher, 109
Bassett, J., 40
Becker, Anne, 9
Beyond with James Van Praagh
  (TV series), 69
  cancellation of, 128
  undercover investigation of,
    120–22
bias
  confirmation, 151–53
    avoiding, 153–54
  double-blind experiments
    eliminate, 158–59
  experimenter, experiments
    disproving, 65
  were flawed, 111–14
Blackmore, S., 113
brain science/scientists, criticism
  of, 19–20
Braude, Stephen E., 22, 24
Buttny, R., 132

Camp Chesterfield, 99, 152, 161
Campbell, Laurie, 60, 68
Carroll, B.E., 39
Carroll, Robert T., 81

channeling, 90
  New Age, 10–11
Chapman, J., 109
Christopher, M., 130
clairvoyant dreams, 74
clients/audiences
  interaction between medium
    and, 132–34
  preparation of, 124
  pressure on, to believe, 105–
    106
closure, 11
cold readings, 81–84, 97, 101, 130
  role of client in, 86–87
  techniques of, 84–86
  use of, by TV psychics,
    122–24
confirmation bias, 151–53
  avoiding, 153–54
Crossing Over (Edward, J.), 104
Crossing Over With John Edward
  (TV series), 11, 92, 119, 122
  cancellation of, 128
  release required of partici-
    pants on, 124–25
cueing, experiments disproving,
  62–63
Cullen, L., 51

daemon, 18
Dale, Lily, 10
Dateline NBC (TV series), 10, 14,
  98
Davenport brothers, 98
Davies, O., 40
death, human curiosity about, 9
deathbed visions, 21
deceased persons
  role of, in Spiritualism, 50–52

Spiritualism offers continuation of relationships between living and, 52–53
see also spirits
Dodds, E.R., 21, 24
Doyle, Arthur Conan, 14
dreams
communication by, 73
interpretation of, 75
types of, 74
Drew, P., 147
Dubois, Alison, 11, 95, 96
Duncan, Helen, 41–42

ectoplasm, 78
Edward, John, 11, 68, 97, 120
criticism of, 100–101, 102–104, 105–106, 108
data supporting living soul hypothesis and, 59–60
on proof of spirit contact, 107
skeptics on, 92
Edward, Mark, 88
evidence
anecdotal, 154–56
religious, 159–60
scientific, 156–58
experimenter bias, experiments disproving, 65
were flawed, 111–14

Faraday, Michael, 151
fishing for details, 84
Fontana, David, 16, 154
Forer, Bertram, 82
fortune-tellers, 16
Fox sisters (Kate and Margaret), 10, 39–40, 98
fraud
mediums refute charges of, 62

public association of mediums with, 42

Galileo, 57
Gauld, Alan, 58
Gehman, Anne, 60, 68
Gellman, Marc, 159
Ghost Whisperer, The (TV series), 69
ghosts, 7
Goffman, E., 132, 134
Goss, R., 51
Greer, Jane, 12
Grodin, Charles, 94, 95

Hart, Hornell, 21
Hayden, Mrs., 40
Hazelgrove, J., 41
Heritage, J., 147
Hockenberry, John, 103
Holt, E., 132
hot readings, 89–90, 101–102
Houdini, Harry, 99, 101–102, 106–107, 107–108
Humphries, S., 42
Hydesville Rappings, 10, 40
Hyman, R., 111, 130

information, vague, experiments disproving, 63–64

James, William, 14
Jaroff, Leon, 92, 102
John Edward Cross Country (TV series), 11
Journal of the Society of Psychical Research, 87

Keenes, M. Lamar, 90, 91, 99, 102, 152
Klass, D., 51
Knight, J.Z., 90

Larry King Live (TV program), 92, 97, 100, 107

Leudar, I., 132

Limoges, Yvonne, 9

living soul hypothesis, 56, 59
    assumptions explaining tests confirming, 59

lucky guesses, experiments disproving, 64

magic wand theory, 22, 23

materialization, 78

Matthews, R., 109

Mayes, P., 132

Medium (TV series), 9, 69, 95

mediums
    answers to skeptics' criticism of, 61–68
    beginning of modern era of, 10
    celebrity, criticism of, 91–94
    cheating by, 160–62
    definition of, 9
    distortion of reality by, 95–96
    experiments validating, 110–11
        bias/selective remembering in, 111–14
        problem with control group in, 114–16
    interaction between client and, 132–34
    mind-reading by, experiments disproving, 66–67
    motivations of, 65–66
        profit as, 91–92
    new breed of, 99–101
    patterns followed by, 135–42
    reasons for learning about, 13–14
    self-deception of, 68
    silence as risk to, 144–46
    spirits work together with, 71–72

use of reported speech by, 131–32
    verbal negotiation with, 45
    verbal strategies of, 146–48

mediumship
    claims of, 130
    definition of, 16
    in history, 18–19
    manifestations of, 17
    passive vs. physical forms of, 44
    in Spiritualist services, 44
    super-ESP argument for, 20–27
    trance, 100

Mediumship and Survival (Gauld), 58

memory, in universe, 67

Menace of Spiritualism, The (O'Donnell), 41

Meynell, K., 40

Mumler, William H., 98

Murphy, Gardner, 21

Myers, G., 132

Nelson, G., 51

Nelson, Lonnie, 109

New Age channelers, 10–11

New York Times Magazine, 105

Nickell, Joe, 97, 154

Northrup, Suzane, 29, 60, 68

Occam's razor, 57

O'Donnell, Elliot, 41

O'Keefe, Ciaran, 109

Omarr, Sydney, 83

O'Neill, Michael, 102

O'Neill, Tom, 152

Oprah Winfrey Show (TV series), 69–70

Other Side, The (TV series), 93
Ouija board, 76–77

Palladino, Eusapia, 161
paraphernalia, of psychics, 16–17
Pascal, Blaise, 57
Phillips, S.U., 132
physical phenomena, 77–78
Plato, 18
Podmore, Frank, 21
poltergeist phenomena, 21
Popoff, Peter, 89
prophecy, prosecution for, 47
prophetic dreams, 74
Psychic Mafia, The (Keenes), 90,
  99, 102, 152
Psychic News, 42
psychics, 16–17
  see also mediums
Puharich, Andrija, 152

Randi, James, 92, 130, 157
red herring fallacy, 160
religion
  Spiritist, 11–12
  as spiritual basis for belief in
    afterlife, 10
  see also Spiritualism
reported speech, 131–32
Rhine, J.B., 21
Richet, Charles, 21
Roberts, Mrs., 40
Roe, C.A., 130
Rowland, Ian, 81, 84, 85, 111
Russek, Linda, 56, 109
Russek Protocol, 88

San Diego Union-Tribune
  (newspaper), 93
Schwartz, Gary E., 56, 87, 96, 109
Sefton, Dru, 93
sensory leakage, 20

lack of safeguards in tests
  disproving, 116–18
Seven Principles, The, 43–44
Shermer, Michael, 12, 90, 153,
  157
  on Van Praagh, 93
sitter-silent condition, 88
Skeptic (magazine), 92
Skeptical Enquirer (magazine),
  119, 120
skeptics
  mediums answers to criticism
    by, 61–68
  motivations of, 66
Skeptic's Dictionary (Carroll,
  R.T.), 81
Socrates, 18–19
spirit writing, 100
Spiritist religion, 11–12
spirits
  communication with, 70–71
    by dreams, 73–75
  concurrent appearances of, in
    different places, 35–37
  inspirational thoughts from,
    75–76
  manifestations of, 73, 77–79
  messages from, 46
    as advice/warnings, 46–47
    as healing energies, 49–50
    of reconciliation, 48–49
  separation between dead
    family members and, 37–38
Spiritualism
  offers continuation of rela-
    tionships, 52–53
  post-WWII decline in, 42–43
  role of deceased in, 50–52
  roots of, 39–40, 98–99
  seven principles of, 43–44
Spiritualist National Union
  (SNU), 40
Supernatural (TV series), 9

Tannen, D., 132
telepathy, 21
television
    mediums on, 9, 11, 91
      are fakes, 127–28
    see also specific programs
Time (magazine), 102, 105
trances, 79, 100
Truzzi, Marcello, 93

Underdown, James, 119

Van Praagh, James, 11, 69, 120

on role of psychics, 90
skeptics on, 92–94

Walliss, John, 39
Why Smart People Believe Weird Things (Shermer), 93, 153
Williams, P.L., 132
Winfrey, Oprah, 69–70
Wiseman, Richard, 109
Witchcraft Act (Britain, 1735), 41–42, 47
Wooffitt, Robin, 129, 132

Young, M., 51